The Story of Queen Mary
MOTHER AND QUEEN

MOTHER AND QUEEN

The Story of Queen Mary

by

MARION CRAWFORD

PRENTICE-HALL, INC. NEW YORK

FIRST AMERICAN EDITION

First printing.........October, 1951
Second printing.....November, 1951

Printed in the United States of America.
Designed by Stefan Salter.

ACKNOWLEDGEMENTS

The publishers gratefully acknowledge the kind permission to use certain material in this book, and record here their thanks: to John Gore, author of the official biography *King George V*, and his publisher, John Murray; to Louis Wulff, author of *Her Majesty Queen Mary*, and his publishers, Sampson Low, Marston and Co., Ltd.; to Miss Kathleen Woodward, author of *Queen Mary*, and her publishers, Hutchinson and Co.; to Eyre and Spottiswoode Ltd., publishers of *Queen Mary*, by the late Sir George Arthur; to Thomas Nelson and Sons, Ltd., publishers of *Life of Her Majesty, Queen Mary*, by the late Sir Clement Kinloch-Cooke.

The Story of Queen Mary
MOTHER AND QUEEN

PART ONE

"IF ever I had to make a decision that would affect me or anyone dependent on me, if ever I were in difficulty or distress of any sort, of all the women in the world, I should go straight to Queen Mary."

That tribute was uttered by a woman whose good fortune it had been to serve Her Majesty, Queen Mary, as Princess, as Duchess, and as Queen, for many years. I repeat it now, at the beginning of my story, because it is as true for me as it is for everyone who has enjoyed the honor and privilege of being associated with Queen Mary.

It must be essentially a love story, not only because it is written in affection, but much more because mutual love between the Royal family and the British people is the keystone of the institution of monarchy as we now know it, and the sufficient explanation of its strength.

And I feel that it is not a story that ought to be begun at the conventional beginning. Birthdays and dates of reigns, jubilees, wars, and other great events may help us to see in some sort of perspective the vast arch of history that her useful life has spanned. But Queen Mary is much more than a figure in an historical pageant; she is a great woman of our time.

Of all my seventeen years as Governess to their Royal Highnesses, the Princess Elizabeth and the Princess Margaret, what now stands out most sharply in my mind and heart is the memory of one historic night—a wild, stormy night of January—that brought home to all of us the depth of our affection for Queen Mary.

Surely all of us who are old enough, remember exactly where we were and what we were doing on the night the news came over the radio that King George V was dying. I have asked many people, and every one remembered. Some spoke of the groups that gathered to kneel in prayer. One friend was at a party in a chalet on a Swiss mountainside; there was no more singing or dancing that night. Another, going ashore in a West Indian port, found Negroes, hatless, kneeling in the street in front of a radio shop.

I was in my mother's house in Dunfermline, where I had gone for my Christmas holiday. We talked far into the night, and there was little sleep for any of us. As I lay in bed, I thought of Queen Mary in her sorrow. Outside, the storm howled.

In the morning came a telegram from the Duchess of York, recalling me to the Royal Lodge at Windsor. I could not reply, because the wires were down; but as soon as I could, I hurried off, to travel all day through the storm to the Royal Lodge, where the Princesses Elizabeth and Margaret were. Their parents, who had gone to London to be with Queen Mary in her bereavement, had left a message for me: "Don't let all this depress them more than is absolutely necessary, Crawfie; they are so young!"

And where had Queen Mary been while the last sad messages went out to the world? Sitting by her husband's side in the red-carpeted bedroom at Sandringham House, the country residence that had been perhaps more truly home to him than any of the castles or palaces. A log fire burned in the grate.

In the morning there had been a Privy Council meeting, attended by the Prince of Wales and the Dukes of York and Kent. When it was over, and the pen with which the King had signed his last document had fallen from his hand, Queen Mary still sat there, all through the long winter afternoon and evening. At night, her sons and her daughter, the Princess Royal, joined her at the bedside. At five minutes before midnight the King died.

All over the Empire, bells were tolled and shops were

closed the next day, in mourning for the Sovereign who in twenty-five years of wise and understanding rule had won such a place in the people's affections. It was hard to imagine what the future would be like without him.

Certainly it would be different, but how different none of us could know.

And while the bells tolled and sermons were preached and statesmen of all nations spoke of the greatness of the dead King and the depth of our loss, everyone who prayed at all must have prayed for Queen Mary, who was Queen of England no longer, but still, in a very special sense, a mother to the British people.

Her thoughts must have gone back forty-two years to the time when, as the young bride of the Duke of York, the Prince of Wales's heir, she had first come to Sandringham. She had come, not to the great country house, but to a smaller dwelling on the grounds, York cottage, where she spent many happy years as a young wife and where five of her children were born.

Truly, the story of Queen Mary is a love story, not only of her love for the British people and theirs for her, but also of the bonds of affection between a woman and her husband and family.

It must have been very soon after my first meeting with Queen Mary, nearly nineteen years ago, that she said to me: "My help at any time is always at your disposal, as you know." Since then I have not hesitated to take my problems to her—and not only the problems that arose in the course of my work, but even the little, everyday difficulties that affected me alone. And she has never failed to be gracious, sympathetic, and actively helpful.

Putting a hand on my shoulder, she would say, "My dear," and then, from the wisdom of her long experience of men, women and things, would give me the advice and encouragement I needed.

When I close my eyes and imagine Queen Mary's voice, the words I hear are "My dear!" They are so characteristic of her, and so full of meaning. They come from the heart of a woman, a wife, and a mother.

To Queen Mary I am indebted for countless acts of kindness. Letters of encouragement, a treasured sprig of white heather that is a memento of one of my first meetings with her, the plan of my cottage garden, the very pictures on my walls speak to me of her kindly interest. It is in gratitude that I am setting out to write about her, not only in the light of my own experience, but also from the testimony of others who have known her.

There are not many books about Queen Mary, and none that traces her life through the whole of eighty-three years in which she has been a beloved figure. For it is not too much to say that she has been beloved from the day of her birth. No more welcome Princess ever came into the world than she who was to be known to the British people as Princess May.

Not long ago, I had a letter from a friend in America: "I have just seen Queen Mary in a news-reel," she wrote, "and I must write and tell you about it. She was at an exhibition, or something of that sort—walking about, dignified, stately and yet lively, and so intensely interested in everything she saw. Someone started to applaud, and that is very unusual in cinemas here. At once, the clapping was taken up, to spread through the whole theatre. And then I heard a woman say, in a voice that seemed to break, but a very American voice: 'Oh, isn't she every inch a Queen!' "

Is it not remarkable that a woman who has never sought the center of the stage, but has always been content to play a self-effacing part, should inspire such a demonstration in a distant land among people not her own?

No doubt that news-reel showed her at the British Industries Fair. We know her way of going to see everything that is worth seeing, of asking just the questions that will bring the most useful answers. We are accustomed to her going to the theater, sometimes twice a week, going to the Oaks and the Derby in the same week, although she does not care much for racing. We hear without surprise that after a long afternoon watching tennis at Wimbledon—which she *does* enjoy—she has a hurried dinner at home and is back at the Center Court by 8.30. At eighty-three years of age, she makes good use of every minute that she is awake; and that is what she has been doing all her life.

Everyone who knows Queen Mary must realize that she is still one of the busiest women alive. In spite of her dislike of the limelight (that endearing shyness which has been with her from girlhood), she is no dim and distant figure, but an extraordinarily vivid personality.

Perhaps it is her own reluctance to speak of herself, or indeed to speak in public at all, that has deterred those who have written about other great women of our time from attempting to write about Queen Mary.

Her voice—a very beautiful voice, by the way—has never been heard on the radio. To have talked with her, to have listened to her, walked with her, driven with her and sat at her table, are privileges that I shall always cherish.

I have heard people say that it is not easy to know Queen Mary, and I think I understand what they mean. Such dignity and reserve could never be penetrated by anyone who had the presumption to set out to do so. These royal qualities come to her naturally, by inheritance, and no one who meets her or even sees her can forget for a moment that she was born a Princess, in the line of Kings.

She has influenced all our lives, even those of us who have never seen her or heard her voice. She is not merely a high-born personage whom we see driving past in her carriage, but one who is close to our hearts. So the Queen who is said to be "not easy to know" is in fact one of the best known women in the world—made known by her character, her acts and her example.

And yet . . . while my story of "The Little Princesses" was appearing in *Woman's Own* magazine, a girl wrote to me:

"Why don't you tell us more about Queen Mary? What you do say about her only makes me want to know more, for she is certainly a marvelous woman. I have tried to find books about her, but they are very scarce. And I have always remembered something that my grandmother once told me about her. Is it true that Queen Mary, before she was married to the late King George, was engaged to another Prince?"

It is true. The death of "Prince Eddy," the Duke of Clarence, eldest son of that Prince of Wales who was to become King Edward VII, was perhaps the first great sorrow in Queen Mary's life.

But isn't it strange that a girl who, as she told me in her letter, treasured albums of pictures of Queen Mary, and read everything she could find in magazines and newspapers about her, was ignorant of the tragedy that had saddened the life of the young Princess and had caused a wave of sympathy to flow out towards her?

And then I recalled that when I was a young girl in Scotland, reading of Queen Mary's visits to Balmoral and her work in the first World War and her part in the events of my time, I myself had never heard a hint of that sorrowful story. Those who adored Princess May as a young woman, by far the most popular young woman of her day, have given place to a generation that reveres Queen Mary as a loving and beloved great-grand-mother.

Yet there is so much more to be told! After a recent garden party at the White Lodge, Richmond Park, where Queen Mary passed a great deal of her girlhood days, a white-haired man of about Queen Mary's own age said to me: "You should have known her when she was a young woman! She was wonderful then, and she is even more wonderful now."

"Princess May" is far more than a lovely legend at Richmond and Kew, where her parents, the Duke and Duchess of Teck, lived so long. Old people there still remember with pride that it was there, in the garden of the White Lodge, that King George V, then Duke of York, asked her to be his wife.

They remember, too, that it was in the drawing room of the White Lodge that Prince Edward, now Duke of Windsor, was christened. And younger people recall that it was to the White Lodge that their present Majesties, King George and Queen Elizabeth, came to live after their marriage.

What memories Queen Mary herself must nurse, not only of the scenes of her girlhood, but also of her happy years as a young wife and mother! And of sad times, too. For surely she has had to bear more than her share of the griefs that so many wives and mothers have suffered in her time.

Of her six children, Prince John died in infancy, the Duke of Kent was killed in an air crash in the course of wartime duty, and Prince Edward, after reigning eleven months, renounced the throne that she and her husband, King George V, had made more respected and admired than it had ever been before.

Indeed, it was by their own devotion to duty, their high ideal of service, and their example, that they made the institution of monarchy in the British Commonwealth so secure that not even the abdication of a King could shake it. Duty must have been Queen Mary's watchword all her life. She has never said so, at least publicly, but has made it apparent in all her acts.

In her fourteen years of widowhood and withdrawal from the active life of the Court, duty has led her into paths that she formerly found difficult to explore. She has found new ways to be useful, and to-day, although she is no longer the first lady in the land, she is even closer to us, and is even better loved, because we can see her more clearly than when she stood as Queen by her husband's side.

There have been many occasions for sadness in Queen Mary's life, but no one can talk with her and listen to her, or see her at work, without realizing that she is a happy woman. And perhaps her happiness lies in the fact that with her the path of duty and the path of love are one and the same.

I would not presume to quote her words on so sacred a matter, but I know that Queen Mary believes that a woman's first duty is to her husband. All her actions show it. And when duty and love lead the same way, there can be no such thing as slavery to duty. Queen Mary has shown it to be the way of true freedom.

She has always made her husband and her home the hub of her universe. It was so before he came to the throne, and then it became clear to all that she was determined to set an example of good family life, and to show herself worthy of him and her own high place. I have spoken with many people who knew her then, thirty years ago, and have learned how great a task she and her husband undertook, and how great were the difficulties they had to overcome.

It may come as a revelation to young people of this generation, and may be hard for them to realize, that there were many misgivings about King George V and Queen Mary at the beginning of their reign.

The King's parents, King Edward VII and Queen Alexandra, had been leaders of a glittering international social circle. Their nine years are still almost legendary as an era of peace and prosperity, fun and games. Or so they seem to some people who can look back so far, although others, less fortunate, may remember that there were hardship and poverty, too.

But King Edward VII and his Queen were certainly popular with all classes of people; and their glory was so bright that it threw into the shadow the quiet, unassuming couple who were to succeed them.

What did the people know of King George V and Queen Mary, except that they were good, upright, family people, absorbed in their work and strictly attentive to their public duties? The King, who had served a long apprenticeship at sea, had become a comfort-loving country gentleman. He had had no chance to show any such dazzling gifts of statesmanship as distinguished his father. King Edward VII, who loved Paris and was in turn loved by the Parisians had brought about the *Entente Cordiale,* the understanding between France and Britain which was a warning to Germany and would surely, it seemed, be a guarantee of peace.

The passing of King Edward VII looked like the end of a good time and the beginning of a drab and puritanical age. People even said that the new couple at Buckingham Palace disapproved of horse-racing; and that, in those days, with the popular Derby victory of King Edward VII's horse "Minoru" still fresh in people's minds, seemed a doleful accusation. There was no more truth in that, of course, than in the much more malicious gossip that went around and was duly disproved. But there was a fairly wide agreement that Britain was in for a dull time.

"Dost thou think," asks someone in a Shakespeare

play, "that because thou art virtuous there shall be no more cakes and ale?" That was what people seemed to be asking the new King and Queen.

If the prophets of gloom had known what Britain and the Empire and the whole world were really in for, they might have shaken their heads even harder. And few could have guessed that what the country needed in the upheavals ahead were the very virtues that King George V and Queen Mary possessed, including some that they had not yet been called on to show.

Over and over again, publicly and privately, King George V said of Queen Mary, "I do not know what I should have done without her." In his very first public speech as King, he said, "I am encouraged by the knowledge that I have in my dear wife a constant helpmate in every endeavour for our peoples' good." Many years later, when he went to Westminster Hall to receive the congratulations of both Houses of Parliament on the occasion of his Jubilee, he was so overcome by emotion when he came to mention the part Queen Mary had played in his life and work that his voice broke and he could hardly finish.

You can hear that on a gramophone record. King George, in preparing the draft of the speech, knew what would happen. "Put that paragraph at the end," he said. "I can't trust myself to speak of the Queen, when I think of all I owe her."

I shall tell of Queen Mary's prodigious memory, of

her wide knowledge of the world and its ways, of her interest in people who "do things," of her uncanny way in conversation of getting at once to the heart of the matter, of her quick, sympathetic understanding of human motives.

All these good feminine qualities and many more were brought to her husband's aid, to support him in his problems, and often to show him the way out of them. Queen Mary brought to her husband, not indeed the ripe wisdom and knowledge that are hers to-day, but an eagerness to learn and to know that had been with her from childhood and is still with her.

Learning came more naturally to her than to him. She had read more than he had, and was quicker to assimilate what she read. As his responsibilities increased, so did his need of her. It was a stern task for him to undertake the long course of deep reading in history and public affairs that he set himself as a young heir to the throne. Dutifully he mastered it, with his wife by his side, already well read, and full of intellectual curiosity which sometimes amused and puzzled him, but always filled him with admiration. Even if the business in hand was only the opening of an exhibition or the laying of a foundation stone, Queen Mary equipped herself beforehand with all the necessary information. She it was who, before they went to India together, collected all the books she could find about the country.

Later, when her son, the future King George VI, went across the Atlantic as a young midshipman in the *Cumberland*, it was Queen Mary who looked up all the books that would be useful to him, searching for those describing the countries he was to visit. As a guide to the West Indies, for example, she recommended Treves's *Cradle of the Deep*. And she gave him books full of facts about Canada and its people.

I shall have a good deal to say about this intellectual curiosity of hers, because I have seen it so often in action. It is as active now as it has always been.

Most of the beautifully bound classics of literature that are in the bookshelves of Princess Elizabeth and Princess Margaret are gifts from Queen Mary. She used to send me a note just before Christmas every year, naming certain books and asking me if I thought the Princesses would like them. One Christmas, for example, a complete set of the Temple edition of Shakespeare arrived, all fitting perfectly in a nice little glass-fronted cabinet which came with them. At other times the Princesses received from Queen Mary the works of Jane Austen, R. L. Stevenson, Dickens, Scott, Byron, Shelley, Keats, Wordsworth, Chaucer and the Letters of Queen Victoria.

King George V, in his diaries and elsewhere, repeatedly acknowledged his good fortune in having such a Consort by his side. Looking back to-day, we all can realize how fortunate we have been to have Queen Mary with us through the years of conflict and ever-recurring crises.

I shall tell of her work in the two great wars, and in the anxious years between. It has been woman's work —not only the work of a woman of high affairs, but also that of a wife and mother.

How proud she must have been of her first son, Edward, who, as soon as the war of 1914 began, went into training with the Grenadier Guards and was in action in France before he was twenty-one!

"What does it matter if I am shot?" he said. "I have four brothers." Surely there was something recklessly prophetic about that. To one of his brothers, he was to resign his throne.

I think Queen Mary's message to the nation, at the time of the abdication, must have brought her right into the hearts of every family in the universe. She said:

"I need not speak to you of the distress which fills a mother's heart when I think that my dear son has deemed it to be his duty to lay down his charge, and that the reign which had begun with so much hope and promise has so suddenly ended."

Only to that diary in which she writes every day, can she have confided her own thoughts during that trying time. I know that I felt drawn closer to her than ever before.

In *The Little Princesses*, I have told what it meant to

them and their parents to be thrust suddenly into a new way of life, and into new and terrifying responsibilities. But about Queen Mary, there is so much more to be told.

She had not only a mother's part to play, but that of a woman who had been Queen, who had been at her husband's side in some of the most dangerous crises that the nation and the throne had had to face, who could bring her wisdom and experience to her family's aid. Loving duty is the tie that binds Queen Mary to them and to all of us.

We know of her never-ending interest in the way the people of Britain live and work. To-day it is a regular thing for the King and Queen to visit workers' homes and factories, to see for themselves how the things we use are made. It was Queen Mary who started all that, long before she was Queen, even before her marriage. As a girl she surprised Court circles by sending for Blue Books of industrial statistics, and then finding out for herself the truth about wages and prices. But as she was then only a junior Princess, this unconventional curiosity did not seem to matter very much.

Queen Mary, later, was to show that it mattered a great deal. King George V had not been on the throne very long before he and his Queen were taking tea with a miner's wife in South Wales, visiting the mines and other industries of Yorkshire, exploring the potteries of Staffordshire, and the railway works at Crewe.

Something new and very fine had been brought to the institution of monarchy in Britain, and far from detracting from the grandeur of Royalty, this something new had increased its strength. But Queen Mary's part in this great achievement is only a portion of the story that I have set myself to tell.

How many people realize that Queen Mary has traveled farther and seen more of the world than any other Queen in history? And what she has seen, she remembers—not only the pageantry of State occasions such as that dazzling Durbar at Delhi which can never be repeated, but also the little intimate incidents that were unrehearsed and have passed almost unrecorded.

Certainly their inner significance was not seen at the time. I want to try to show them, and a thousand other incidents, encounters and actions, as details in the great picture that covers more than eighty-three eventful years.

I have often been with Queen Mary when she was at work making the wonderful carpet in *gros point* that she made to be sold in America as a contribution to the dollar export drive; and I thought of that other English Queen of long ago, working at her spinning wheel or at a piece of tapestry, while her ladies sang to her. Queen Mary usually had her lady-in-waiting read to her while she worked; neither her hands nor her mind are ever idle.

And, watching her, talking with her, listening to her

while she worked, I felt that there was something wonderfully symbolic in the way she went about that womanly task. The pictures she was making were not historic scenes of chivalry and heraldry, but flowers.

That set me thinking of her love of flowers, of Queen Mary's rose garden in Regent's Park, of her visits to the Chelsea Flower Show, of her delight in cottage gardens as well as the Royal gardens at Windsor, and of the flower paintings that she gave me for the wall of my own cottage.

Indeed, the more I have seen of Queen Mary and the more I have heard and read of her, the more I have wanted to write about her.

```
┌─────────────────────┐
│                     │
│    PART TWO         │
│                     │
└─────────────────────┘
```

WHEN you see Queen Mary's Standard flying over Marlborough House (the square-fronted, red brick building which faces St. James's Park, across the Mall—within sight of Buckingham Palace), you know that Queen Mary is at home. Take notice of that Standard, for it is a record of proud history. Its quarterings, full of meaning to those who can read the noble language of heraldry, tell of Queen Mary's descent from King George III and the princely House of Teck.

Marlborough House, most homelike of the royal residences, is truly home to Queen Mary. She knew it first when, as a little girl, she was taken there from Kensington Palace to play with her young relatives, the children of Edward Prince of Wales, Queen Victoria's son. One of them became her husband, and it was at Marlborough

House that they lived as Prince and Princess of Wales for eight years.

After King George V died, Queen Mary went back to the old home, and stayed there until the outbreak of war. The house was not extensively damaged, but bomb-blasts brought down several ceilings.

For a time, some of the rooms were used to house distinguished refugees. But at last it was made ready for Queen Mary to live in again, and one of the first tasks was to arrange her collections of antiques and other beautiful things.

To-day, with its crystal chandeliers, gold frescoed ceilings, deep-pile crimson carpets, tapestries and royal portraits, Marlborough House is far more glorious within than without. Queen Mary's bedroom, boudoir, sitting rooms and private dining room are on the first floor, overlooking the garden and the Mall.

Almost any afternoon or evening when Queen Mary's Standard is flying, if you stand in the Mall and wait a little while, you may be lucky enough to see a big, ancient but well-kept and unmistakably Royal car come through the gates. Sitting erect, and well forward in the body of the limousine, so that she can see and be seen, Queen Mary acknowledges salutes with a gracious inclination of her head.

I have often waited there, not indeed in the hope of seeing Her Majesty pass through the gates in her motor car, but in the certainty that in a few minutes, at a very precise moment, I should be walking through the gates and in at the front door, in response to Queen Mary's kind invitation to "take tea with her."

You can well imagine how happy I was to receive such an invitation, and not only because it came from a Queen, but also because I knew that I should enjoy an hour or so of wise and stimulating conversation.

The invitation was always in the same form. A note would come to me at Buckingham Palace from Queen Mary, to say that she would like me to come to Marlborough House to tea at 5 p.m. on a certain day. She hoped that this would be convenient, and would I please telephone at once to her lady-in-waiting. I would do so, and also make a special note of the date in my engagement book.

This preciseness is very characteristic of Queen Mary. She is never late for any engagement, public or private, and she expects the same punctuality from others. Not many of us would like all our goings and comings to be regulated by the clock, and planned for days ahead; but that is how Queen Mary lives, and I believe that she enjoys that way of living. It conforms with her ideal of duty. From her earliest childhood she has known that she was born to work, and has trained herself to make the best use of every moment of each day.

Herself the soul of punctuality, Queen Mary likes to have all communications acknowledged at once. I have known her lady-in-waiting to ring me at Buckingham Palace to ask whether I had received a letter which

Queen Mary had sent me by hand only two hours before. Not that there was any likelihood of any letter of hers lying unrecognised and unopened. The name "Queen Mary" was always at the lower left-hand corner of the envelope. It was as if she had set out from the beginning to keep a record of every moment of her life —not to aid her own uncannily accurate memory, but to make matters easy for others.

On the appointed day I would dress with great care. Queen Mary herself is so exquisitely dressed that I always felt that nothing but my very best would do on these occasions. It is now nearly nineteen years since my first meeting with her, and I have never seen her in a dress that looked as if it had been worn more than once.

She always looks as if she has just "stepped out of a bandbox." Her clothes never show the slightest crease, one reason being that she never lounges in a chair, but always sits upright. And she prefers a hard chair.

Queen Mary's clothes reflect her own steadfastness of style and character. It is not stiffness, but certainly it is dignity, and by her clever use of color she manages to achieve variety too. Everyone must have noticed her love of delicate pastel shades. She avoids black, probably because she has had to wear black so often at periods of mourning for near and distant relatives. Later, when I come to write about her early life, you may see why black is so distasteful to her.

As a young woman she was wise enough to save up all

the lovely brocades and silks that came to her as presents from the ends of the earth. Stored in boxes and carefully catalogued, they have been drawn on for use as she needed them; so that the dress she wears to-day, looking so new and fresh, may easily have been made from material that she had treasured for many years.

That is as true of the magnificent evening dresses, encrusted with jewels, that she wears on state occasions, as of the informal suits and dresses in which she goes shopping, or pays everyday visits.

So when I dressed to go to tea with Queen Mary I took care to avoid black; and I was more than careful to be punctual. I would lay out all my things on my bed —flawless stockings, gloves, handkerchiefs, handbag and shoes. Then I would give myself plenty of time to dress.

Buckingham Palace is only five minutes' walk from Marlborough House, but I always had a haunting fear of being late. Anything, I felt, might happen in that short walk. A street accident, a parade in the Mall, with streets cordoned off. Nothing of the sort ever did happen, but I never felt quite sure that it wouldn't.

I would leave the Palace at 4.40 p.m., and exactly at 4.45 p.m. would be standing in the Mall, looking at the gates of Marlborough House, and at Queen Mary's Standard flying above. The flag seemed to have a special message for me; Queen Mary was at home, expecting me for tea!

I used to be a little angry with myself for being so

early, but I could not help it. Then began a routine that never varied. I would gaze across the Mall to the clock on St. James's Palace to make sure that I had made no mistake in the time. Then I would make sure that the gates of Marlborough House were still there, with the sentry and the policeman in their places. Reassured, but still a little anxious, I would turn and walk slowly up St. James's Street, to stop always at a shop-window, whose contents I knew by heart.

It was a fascinating window, filled with elaborate fishing tackle that gladdened my Scottish eyes, and set me dreaming—with one eye on the clock—of the burns and the glens that I loved. There was a gaily colored salmon fly that I gazed at with delight, counting the minutes as they passed.

At 4.50 p.m. precisely I would walk down St. James's Street, across the Mall and into the gateway of Marlborough House, where the policeman, who knew me, and was expecting me, would wave me on. Then slowly I would walk round the short, curving drive to the front door, which swung open as I came to it, at five minutes to five.

Not until the door was quite open would I see the uniformed footman, who took my coat and carried it as we walked along the corridor, remarking what a nice or nasty day it was for the time of the year.

A long, elegant, straight staircase led up to Queen Mary's private rooms. At the top of the staircase, waiting for me, was Queen Mary's own personal footman, a charming man of quiet dignity, who always welcomed me with a courtly smile.

As I put my foot on the top step, the clock on St. James's Palace would strike five very solemnly, and the footman's eyes and mine would meet in silent appreciation of my perfect timing. As the last stroke of five died away he would say, "Her Majesty is waiting"—upon which he would open the door to the sitting room where Queen Mary stood, facing me.

I would curtsy to her as soon as I entered the room. Then this smiling, gracious lady would step forward to welcome me with a handshake. I would curtsy again and kiss her hand, with which she raised me so that she could kiss my cheek. A third curtsy completed the formal but to me very delightful greeting.

"Let us have tea first, and then we can have a talk," Queen Mary would say, walking with me from the sitting room, hung with grey-blue silk, to a smaller and very lovely room where tea had been laid on a little round table. In summer this table stood near a window, in winter near the fire.

Queen Mary's tea table, although I saw it often, never failed to give me a thrill of pleasure as soon as I entered the room. The table was covered with an exquisite linen cloth, edged with lace; the cups, saucers and plates were of a beautiful blush-rose shade; the knives and teaspoons were of mauve-pink enamel on silver.

I can picture the table so clearly now. Nothing was ever changed on it, the fare always the same—a dishful of scones and muffins, and a cake. I would stand beside the table for a moment while Queen Mary made the tea; this she always did before she sat down.

In the middle of this preparation she would say, "Do sit down, my dear." Then we would both be seated. Boiling water came from a silver kettle hanging over a methylated spirit lamp. The kettle, like many other objects in that and other rooms of Marlborough House, bore the monogram v.r.—(for VICTORIA REGINA.)

We would eat hot scones and cake, using small silver and enamel forks. Halfway through tea, Queen Mary would refill the teapot from the kettle, and take from the tray a curious instrument—a slender silver pipe, nine or ten inches long, funnel-shaped at one end. Blowing down this pipe, she would put out the blue flame under the kettle. Perhaps that blow-pipe was Queen Victoria's too. With the firelight flickering on the silver kettle, it was easy to imagine that we were back in the Victorian age.

There was always a feeling of permanence, of stability, in that little room. It could have been Queen Victoria, instead of the poet, Rupert Brooke, who asked, "And are there muffins still for tea?"

Queen Mary's movements and gestures, too, were graceful in a way that is seldom seen to-day. Taking tea with her was always a very charming experience.

After tea we talked for an hour or more, but never of the past. The Victorian illusion vanished as Queen Mary, with her alert mind alive to the facts of to-day, spoke of plays, books, motion pictures and people. She loves to talk of the play she has just seen or read. She is greatly interested in what the critics have to say about it, and they would be surprised to hear the excellent criticism of so discerning a playgoer as Queen Mary.

Her experience of the theater goes back a long way. As Duchess of York she saw many of the outstanding plays of the 'nineties, and her eyes light up when she hears tunes from "The Geisha" or "The Belle of New York." During the reign of George V her theater-going was necessarily restricted, but in later years she had taken full advantage of her greater freedom from official duties to make private, informal visits to theaters and movies. She probably knows more about modern plays and films than any other member of the Royal Family.

From the tea-room we would go back to the sitting room for a real discussion of many subjects, the uppermost one being the education of her grand-daughters.

Nearly always I had come eager to consult her concerning some point that had arisen in connection with their lessons. A change in the schoolroom time-table, for example. When the present King and Queen came to the throne, it seemed clear that the change in the position of the Princesses called for alterations in their training, and it was at the Queen's request that I had sent

Princess Elizabeth's school time-table to Queen Mary; and so it became almost a matter of course that I should go to her for advice. Whenever I felt the responsibility too heavy for me alone, I found a wonderful ally in Queen Mary.

Often after tea we spent half an hour or so in drawing up lists of places of historical interest that Queen Mary had planned to take the children to see. At about six o'clock she would rise and say how nice it was to have had a talk. And then I would curtsy again and depart, thinking on the way back to the Palace of the plans for the next of Queen Mary's outings for the children.

They were what we called "the little excursions" which. Queen Mary, the Little Princesses and I, made every Monday afternoon for several years.

I used to receive a little note, saying that Queen Mary would arrive at the Palace at two o'clock. The children and I would have a quick lunch at the Palace, then rush to get ready. At 2 o'clock precisely we would be whisked off with Queen Mary in her car to see something old or new, but always wonderful. On the way, the Princesses would chatter, as eagerly as any other children, of the marvels they were going to witness. On one occasion, I remember Princess Margaret asking, "Shall we see the block where they used to chop the heads off?" But that wasn't the day for our visit to the Tower of London.

Princess Elizabeth and Princess Margaret were just

as excited by the mechanical models in the Science Museum at South Kensington. I well remember Queen Mary pushing the buttons on the glass cases. She got every bit as much enjoyment as the two little girls, from seeing the wheels go round and the models begin to work.

"Oh, Grannie, come and see this!" the children would cry. "Look at what I've found."

The South Kensington Museums were, I think, our happiest hunting ground. I have met Londoners who have never entered these wonderful places, and do not know how fortunate London is to have them.

At one museum, on a very warm afternoon, we climbed many stairs to inspect the fierce heads of countless lions and tigers in cases. Queen Mary seemed more than usually interested in a group of heads of tigers which had been shot by King George V and presented to the Museum. She seemed very thoughtful and a little puzzled as she looked from one to another of the heads. At last she said:

"But shouldn't there be another one here? A particularly fine tiger?"

After much searching and questioning it was discovered that the head had been taken down to be de-mothed and cleaned. That episode filled the curator and me with real admiration. All those tigers looked exactly alike to me. I should not have missed an absentee in a hundred visits.

I remember the memorable day when Queen Mary took us to see the beautiful Painted Hall at Greenwich. The children were more excited than usual because they enjoyed the long ride through London streets. The day was lovely, and when I saw Greenwich, with the wise old Thames flowing silently by, I thought how right they were to call it liquid history. And I exclaimed, "What a wonderful country we live in."

How lucky I was to be with Queen Mary and the Princesses, seeing for the first time places in which Britain's greatness had been founded! And how lucky the Princesses were to have this opportunity of learning history in this unforgettable way!

In the Painted Hall, scaffolding had been erected and artists were busy retouching and cleaning the magnificent murals. Queen Mary led us out to an old cobbled court and placed the tip of her umbrella on the very stones where Sir Walter Raleigh, that clever courtier, was said to have laid his cloak over a puddle for Queen Elizabeth to step on. The children, for once, were silent for a moment. Even Princess Margaret was overawed. "Why," said Princess Elizabeth, "there's a little hollow, even now." And there was.

One afternoon, at the Tower of London, we visited the Governor and were shown the beautiful black oak table at which Raleigh had dined while he was a prisoner in the Tower, after his fall from favor. We held our breath while we traced with our fingers his initials, carved by his own hand on the table.

On the same day, while we were being shown the dungeon in which the saintly Thomas More spent the last months of his life, Princess Margaret discovered a small inner cell. While the others were talking, she led me into the darkness. Suddenly she gave a little yelp of fright and clung to me. Before us was one of those large, stuffed heads of Highland cattle, with long horns which shone in the light from the opening of the cell. The fright was soon over, and as we came out of the cell, faster than we had gone in, we were trying not to laugh.

Princess Margaret was never content to listen; she had to explore on her own. Princess Elizabeth was interested in everything that was shown to us, but Princess Margaret at the time was too young to get excited over such things as the technical details of machines and mechanical processes.

She would wander around and find amusement elsewhere. A boomerang, or, better still, a mummy, could so enchant her that it kept her silent and still; and her silence and stillness were so noticeable that I had to go and see what she had found.

Queen Mary has a remarkable faculty for understanding how things work. It is part of the thoroughness that is second nature to her. The King and Princess Elizabeth have a large share of it, but Princess Margaret, at least as a child, was not so interested in such matters.

We spent one happy afternoon at the Mint, where money ran along a moving belt, counted itself into bags, tied itself up and sprang into a basket on wheels. Queen Mary wanted to know, step by step, just how it all was done. She listened intently while an official explained.

"Thank you," she said. "Now I understand perfectly." There, then, was one more acquisition to the store of knowledge that she has been accumulating all her life.

This visit was just before the Coronation, and we were able to see King George VI's Great Seal being made. A large number of commemorative crown pieces were being minted, and we were told that the delicacy and precision of the machine were so fine that it could engrave on a coin even a hair from a head. Even Princess Margaret was interested.

"I have never been bored in my life," said Queen Mary once to a friend. Perhaps that is why she never seems to get tired, even at eighty-three.

When she was seventy-six, she walked up 144 steps to the top of the high tower at Hawkesbury, which is the Memorial to General Lord Edward Somerset, and, after admiring the view, walked calmly down.

After three hours in exploring a museum or some other place of interest on one of our Monday afternoons, the Princesses and I were glad to rest—but not Queen Mary. Back at the Privy Purse door of Buckingham Palace, the children would curtsy to Queen Mary, kiss her cheek and then her hand. Then, as we got ready to totter upstairs, weary after so much walking and sight-seeing, Queen Mary would turn to her equerry and we would hear her tell him to take her to a Bond Street gallery or some other place where she had an engage-ment—and to arrange to get her back in time for the next one.

People may wonder how the Royal Family can keep up with their endless round of duties. The answer is that this is the task for which they were born and trained. To accept the task and master it is to be in-deed royal. Princesses see their parents going off to functions, day after day, and they know that this will also be their way of living when they grow up.

The path of duty was even narrower when Queen Mary was a child than it is to-day. Children then had to study all day long. There were no light interludes, none of the distractions of the radio, physical culture classes, informal parties, swimming, dancing and friendly games.

Nowadays, much of the best school work is done, not in the schoolroom, but while walking about. Queen Mary, with mind trained to be always taking in new knowledge, new ideas, was eager that the Princesses should see for themselves as much as possible of all the good work that was going on in the world.

Once, in the course of duty, Queen Mary was riding in her car when it was struck by a lorry and turned on its side. The first thing Queen Mary then asked for, when she was helped to climb through the broken windows, and before her bruises were attended to, was a cup of tea.

I have written to-day of Queen Mary as I came to know her while the Little Princesses were growing up. These few years cover only a small part of the long story that I have to tell. But before I go any farther I should like to recall my first meetings with Queen Mary.

To meet a Queen for the first time must be an ordeal for anyone, even for the girl who has been brought up to expect to be presented at Court. A delightful thrill, no doubt, but an ordeal nevertheless. She may lie awake at night, wondering how she will look and behave, trying to remember the right things to do and say and, above all, praying that she will curtsy properly, with left knee bent, back straight, head up, making a deep and graceful obeisance, without hesitation or stumbling. Some girls go to school to learn how it is done, for curtsying is an art, like dancing.

I had no such instruction or practice in preparation for my first meeting with Queen Mary. In my wildest dreams as a schoolgirl, I had never imagined myself being presented to a Queen. Palaces and royal personages were far away from my life in the Ayrshire cottage where I was born, from Moray House Training College, Edinburgh, where I had studied, and from the houses which I had seen during my studies in the poorer districts of Edinburgh, where the sight of poverty had fired me with the ambition to teach.

Perhaps it was as well for me that my first meeting with Queen Mary took place, not in the glittering State room of a palace, but in a lovely English garden, on a Sunday afternoon in late Spring.

It was at the Royal Lodge, the beautiful but unpretentious country house in Windsor Great Park, which is the King's private property, that has always been for King George VI and Queen Elizabeth a pleasant place of retreat from the cares of palace and court. It must be even more so for them now than it was when they were Duke and Duchess of York, and King George V and Queen Mary were on the throne.

There are no sentries, no equerries, no ladies-in-waiting at Royal Lodge. Formerly planned as a shooting lodge for George IV, it has been so modernized that little of the original building, beside the drawing-room, an octagonal room, and the wine cellar, is recognizable.

For a royal residence it is quite small. Painted pink —because Queen Elizabeth cherishes happy thoughts of the pink house where she lived and played as a child— and surrounded by woods, shrubberies, lawns and flower gardens, it fits prettily into the countryside, more than a mile from the grey bulk of Windsor Castle. To me it seemed altogether charming, and its simplicity must appeal even more strongly to those who must spend most of their days in great houses.

In my travels and in reading history, I have often been struck by the fondness of Kings, Queens and Princesses for little houses and little rooms, as quiet refuges from the imposing castles and palaces to which their official duties call them.

There is, at Versailles, the Petit Trianon with its tiny rooms; built for Marie Antoinette so she could play at being a simple country girl. If you have visited the Palace of Holyroodhouse in Edinburgh, you must have noticed how un-palace-like are the cosily small private apartments of Mary, Queen of Scots.

Princesses love dolls' houses. Queen Mary's at Windsor Castle is famous; books have been written about it. Queen Victoria's dolls' house, a marvel in miniature, is often shown to the public at Kensington Palace. I remember well how enchanted the little Princesses were, and Queen Mary as well, when she took them to see the model village at Bekonscot, where every house is a doll's house and the streets are less than a yard wide.

One of the first things Princess Elizabeth wished me to see, on the very day after my arrival at the Royal Lodge to begin my duties, was the "Little House" in the garden, the gift of the people of Wales and the favorite toy of both the Princesses.

It was only a few days after that, when everything was still new and strange to me, that the Duchess gave me the news that King George and Queen Mary were coming to tea on the following Sunday. This was great news, as such visits were infrequent, and from the Duchess's tone and from the air of expectancy that spread through the house, I realized that a Sunday afternoon call of that sort was not in the ordinary course of events. And I realized, too, that I was deeply concerned in the business—that one object of Their Majesties' visit was to see what sort of person I was, to be entrusted with the important task of the education of the two Princesses, then both very young.

I was twenty-two, and I knew that some people had been saying that I was too young for the job. The Duchess had tried to reassure me on this point, telling me that she and the Duke were agreed that a girl of my age, young enough to share the children's interests, and to play as well as work with them, would be a happier companion for them than someone a generation or more removed from them. Still, I felt that I was on trial, and the trial was not one-sided. Had not the Duchess invited me to come "to see how we suit each other?"

Although I was charmed by everything at Royal Lodge, I still had a feeling of living in a fairy-tale that would soon come to an end. Besides, I still felt the pull of the career that I had planned for myself.

That Sunday afternoon will remain in my memory as long as I live.

No hint had been given me of the exact time when Their Majesties would arrive, how or where I should be presented to them or what I should wear—and to tell the truth my dresses were then so few that there was little choice.

That day I wore a simple dress of blue tweed that I had brought from home. Usually on a Sunday afternoon the children walked or played in the garden after lunch, but this time they stayed in the house, so that I found I should have an hour or so—I did not know exactly how long—to spend alone.

I walked in the woods, trying to picture myself being presented to the King and Queen, rehearsing my answers to the questions that I imagined they would ask, and, above all, teaching myself to curtsy.

In the woods I went from tree to tree, curtsying low before each of them, murmuring "Your Majesty," "Sir" and "Ma'am." Not because I was satisfied with my performance, but because I felt Their Majesties might arrive at any moment and it was about time for me to return to the house, I hurried out of the wood and was on the edge of the lawn when I saw two unmistakable figures, both watching me. King George and Queen Mary, alone.

Suddenly I felt more lonely than I had ever felt in my life before. Had they seen me curtsying to the trees? Had I ruined the good impression I dutifully hoped to make on them?

Whatever could have been the answer to those questions, it was clear that I must not hesitate, but must go forward to meet Their Majesties. And I am sure now that what banished my stage fright and made me bold was the sweet smile on the face of Queen Mary.

It was the smile of friendly greeting (that I have seen so often since, on public and private occasions) that I shall have to describe. I have often been given cause to be grateful to Queen Mary, but never more than on that afternoon when she put a young girl at her ease with a gracious smile.

Queen Mary looked truly regal in a pale blue dress and coat, grey gloves and a grey toque with blue feathers. She carried a long grey umbrella with a carved handle of ivory. Her jewels were pearls, and, as brooch and earrings, some of the most beautiful aquamarines I had ever seen. The King was in country tweeds, with soft hat and a walking stick.

"You are Miss Crawford," he said, and I curtsied low to him, then to Queen Mary. I thought what a wonderful couple they made, standing there in that lovely garden.

They talked to me of the children, and of how the garden was growing, making conversation easy for me while, as I was sure, they took stock of me. If they were disappointed in my youthfulness, and would have preferred someone older and more stiff in manner, they showed no sign of it.

The King's deep voice, rather louder that I had expected but not at all terrifying, was that of a country gentleman. He spoke slowly, in an accent that was refreshingly different from the fashionable Metropolitan speech that had seemed so strange, at first, to my Northern ears. All my qualms evaporated during our short conversation.

The Duke and Duchess joined us, with the children. As they all turned and went into the house, I noticed that Queen Mary carried no handbag. That alone would have been a mark of distinction in an age when few women know what to do with their hands unless they have a bag to hold. Queen Mary always insists on having her hands free for the proper disposal of gloves and parasol, and for greetings. How many women can look graceful without a handbag? And how many, without a handbag, can contrive always to look as if they had just left the dressing-table? Queen Mary makes discreet use of lipstick and powder, but if you ask me how she keeps spick and span all day long, without a handbag, I can only reply that it is part of the grand manner.

It was early Spring when I met Queen Mary for the first time. A few days later, while I was still at the Royal Lodge, I was told that "of course" I should be at Princess Elizabeth's sixth birthday party. To me it was by no means a matter of course, but a very exciting event. The prospect of meeting nearly every member of the Royal Family at Windsor Castle itself made my heart beat fast. But under the friendly eyes of Queen Mary and the Duchess of York (as Queen Elizabeth was then), I soon felt that there was nothing to be afraid of.

They presented me to their relatives in the Red Drawing Room. Then the birthday cake was cut, and the six-year-old Princess touched me deeply by bringing over to me a favor from the cake—a small spray of white heather. It was a beautiful gesture, for we had known each other only a few weeks.

Queen Mary watched Princess Elizabeth with a quiet smile. Our eyes met, and I felt that Queen Mary was accepting me, as her little granddaughter already had done.

I still have that spray of heather, tied with pink ribbon.

MEETING Queen Mary, talking with her, seeing her at work and at leisure, on great public occasions and in the intimacy of her home, I found one thought occurring to me, over and over again.

If she had not been born a Princess, she could have chosen almost any career for herself, even in an age when careers for women were far fewer than they are to-day. And she would have been brilliantly successful in whatever field of endeavour she chose.

That thought must have struck a great many other people as well as me. Officials at museums and other places of interest to which we took the little Princesses were surprised by Queen Mary's ready grasp of facts, their background and implications. Statesmen have marvelled at her knowledge of their craft and of their problems. Engineers have been impressed by her eagerness to know the workings of the mechanism they controlled, and librarians by her searching questions and her quick understanding.

The truth is that she has been a student and a worker all her life—and she still is. I cherish a letter that she wrote to me just a few years ago, when Princess Margaret was seventeen. In it, Queen Mary looks back to the time when she herself was seventeen, and writes of her realization then of how much there is to learn in life. She is now, and has always been, interested in *new* things.

Isn't it good to see a woman in her eighties recalling vividly and happily how she felt when she was seventeen! Now, at eighty-three, she is as eager as ever for new and useful knowledge, and as ready to enjoy the freshness of it. We saw her at the British Industries Fair recently, untired after hours of walking, questioning, learning; and at the Chelsea Flower Show, carrying out with relish a tour that would have sent home, tired out, many a woman half her age.

Her great store of physical strength was a constant source of wonder and admiration to her husband, King George V. Once, when Mr. Baldwin, then Prime Minister, congratulated His Majesty on looking well after an illness, he replied: "Yes: I feel pretty well again, but not well enough to walk with the Queen round the British Industries Fair."

Now people may say that it is only natural that Queen Mary, "with all her advantages," should be well educated and well informed, and fitted by her training to show interest in every new thing she saw. But let us examine those advantages and see what they really amounted to.

True, she was born in a Palace, but that could easily have become rather a handicap than an advantage. Princesses have been known to take their futures for granted, to go through life easily, giving little and taking all the good things that came their way, simply because they were born in palaces. Few good things, in a material sense, came the way of Queen Mary in her early years as Princess May. The large, not too comfortable suite of rooms that her mother, Princess Mary, Duchess of Teck, had to live in at Kensington Palace was expensive to run, and no allowance went with it or the other royal residence, White Lodge at Richmond, which also was granted to Queen Mary's parents by Queen Victoria.

My own home, Nottingham Cottage, granted to me on my marriage and for my lifetime by the grace and favor of His Majesty, King George VI, is in the grounds of Kensington Palace, and reached by way of a private road.

Queen Mary, visiting me here, has often spoken to me of her childhood days, when she came here, "just across the way," to see an old retainer who occupied the cottage at the time. The cottage, like Kensington Palace, was built by Sir Christopher Wren, who lived in a neighboring cottage while he was planning the rebuilding of the Palace. But in the reign of King William III, Wren had other tastes to please than his own.

Kensington Palace is certainly not one of Wren's masterpieces. The brickwork is said to be remarkably good, as brickwork, but nobody has ever called the Palace picturesque. Nevertheless, two English Queens, Victoria and Mary, were born there, and perhaps Queen Elizabeth played in these very grounds, for there is an old tradition which says that in the time of Henry VIII, Elizabeth's father, there was a royal nursery on the site.

"Windsor Castle," said Leigh Hunt, the Victorian wit, "is a place to receive monarchs in, Buckingham Palace to see fashion in, and Kensington Palace seems a place to drink tea in." To-day it is a show place, with many rooms open to the public, and for most of the thousands who visit it daily the chief interest, nowadays, in Kensington Palace is that Queen Mary was born there.

Before William III's time, a house stood there. The Earl of Nottingham sold it to the King, who had it rebuilt and enlarged to his own ideas, the result being a regular Dutch Palace in a Dutch garden.

He and his Queen Mary spent the rest of their lives there, and then came Queen Anne, "sitting in quiet stupidity with her fan in her mouth, waiting so anxiously for dinner to be announced and scarcely speaking three words at a time to anybody, while through her court moved Swift, Addison, Steele, and others whose very names give luster to the story of her reign."

Yes, Kensington Palace has seen a lot of history. Here came the dashing Sarah Jennings, afterwards Duchess of Marlborough, Winston Churchill's ancestress, who knew so expertly how to manage her royal mistress. She managed her so well that they dropped all titles, dignities, and formalities and called each other Mrs. Morley and Mrs. Freeman.

We may be sure that our own beloved Queen Mary knows everything there is to be known about Kensington Palace, as she does about all the royal residences. And not only royal residences, but also the homes of British people, and their ways of living and working.

There was great popular rejoicing when she was born on May 26, 1867, but not altogether because, as a great-granddaughter of George III, she stood in the line of succession to the throne. Some commentators pointed out that she had arrived just in time to be a future friend and playmate of her young relations, the sons of the Prince and Princess of Wales; but few can then have thought of her as the future Queen of England. But possibly Queen Victoria did.

I have often thought, in reading Queen Victoria's diaries, that the old lady felt that Fate had marked out the little Princess for her high destiny.

She must have been a beautiful child. Queen Victoria,

who was no indiscriminate admirer of Royal babies' looks, brought herself to write enthusiastically of "the deepest blue eyes imaginable, a tiny rosebud of a mouth, a lovely complexion (pink and white), and a most perfect figure." The baby was one year old then, but even when she was only one month old she had delighted the Queen's eyes. It was Victoria's first sight of her. "At half past five," she wrote, "drove in the open carriage and four through the densely crowded park to Kensington Palace to see dear Mary Teck. It seemed strange to drive into the old courtyard and get out at the door, the very knockers of which were old friends. . . .

"We went up to the very top of the house, and here, in the very bedroom in which Mamma and I had slept, I found dear Mary, Aunt Cambridge, and the baby, a very fine one, with pretty little features and a quantity of fair hair. It is to be called Agnes Augusta Victoria Mary Louise Olga Pauline Claudine. . . . I am to be one of the godmothers."

That remark explains why, at the christening, the name Victoria was put first. The little Princess was soon called Victoria Mary for short, then it became known that her mother called her May, and soon she was "Princess May" to everyone.

To the people, May was "the English Princess," the daughter of the truly English Duchess of Teck, whom everyone loved, whose wit, charm, and happy spirits glowed like sunshine in a court which, in the opinion of many, was unbearably dull.

Queen Victoria at the time was deep in the retirement to which she had condemned herself after the death of the Prince Consort, and the public saw little of her. But her letters and diaries, and the memories of all who were close to her, show that she did not make others suffer by her own tragedy, but hid her grief and turned a pleasant face to those she met. Especially she loved children, loved to see them and play with them. Her diaries are sprinkled with references to her grandchildren and their young friends, among whom, from the beginning, Princess May was a favorite.

I find in the sharp eye for detail that Victoria's diaries reveal, something of the same keen sense of history that is evident in all that Queen Mary says and does. Her memory for little things has always been extraordinarily sharp, and the details are all linked together by the constant realization that she is living history, that she knows where she stands in relation to the past and the future.

A long time ago, at the Coronation of King Edward VII, she was seen to be watching everything with a peculiarly intense expression. A friend asked her later what she had been thinking about, and she replied solemnly: "What it all meant—of the past." And she has tried to pass on that historical sense to her children and her grandchildren. She has often told me how desirous she was that the little Princesses should have a sound historical background, and so should understand their own responsibilities and duties. Especially she wanted them to know the dates in their history books.

Some modern educators try to tell us that dates are of little importance, but Queen Mary believes that they are too useful to be disregarded. "They are a great help," she said to me more than once. "You can fit in and place innumerable pieces of knowledge if you are sound on dates."

Later, when the late Sir Henry Marten, then Provost of Eton, took Princess Elizabeth for instruction in Constitutional History, he was delighted to find that she remembered all the important dates. He told her that some of the bright boys at Eton College could name all the Kings of England, with their dates, in so many seconds. Princess Elizabeth made up her mind to beat this record, and she did.

Queen Mary sent Princess Elizabeth a colored picture showing all the Kings and Queens set out in rows, with names and dates underneath. The Queen Mother had used this herself as a child, and she never regretted having to learn those essential facts.

This picture no doubt will hang again in another schoolroom at Clarence House, before long. Another aid to memory that Queen Mary handed on to her grandchildren was a set of history games, played on the lines of "Happy Families," with the Plontagenets, Tudors, Stuarts, and Hanoverians as the Families. Yellow with age, but still beautiful, these cards have amused and instructed royal children for generations, and no doubt will go on doing so. For they certainly have been put carefully away in a place where they can easily be found when needed. Nothing is surer than that Queen Mary will ask for them one day, and expect them to be produced.

That phenomenal memory of hers is part of her historical background. I well remember how, when her son became King and he and Queen Elizabeth took up residence in Buckingham Palace, Queen Mary very kindly lent to Princess Elizabeth a desk and a bookcase which the people of Edinburgh had presented to King George V and Queen Mary on their marriage.

This desk and bookcase remained in the Buckingham Palace schoolroom for many years until one day I decided that we could do without the desk, as Princess Elizabeth had by this time her own private sitting room, and I never used the desk. So I suggested that it could be put in the store-room. The Princess agreed, but added quickly: "Of course, Crawfie, next time Grannie comes here she is going to say at once, 'Where is the desk?' " Nevertheless we moved it. Months slipped by, and I forgot about it, if the Princess did not. One day I heard quick footsteps in the corridor. Princess Elizabeth dashed into my room, looking flushed and with a twinkle in her eye.

"Crawfie!" she cried. "The desk, quick! Grannie is halfway down the corridor." Then she dashed out.

A few seconds later Queen Mary entered my room, with two smiling Princesses, their eyes full of mischief and mirth, behind her. The Queen Mother and I greeted each other, and then she looked slowly round the room. I felt the question coming. I had hardly time to finish my own thought when Queen Mary said:

"Oh, Crawfie, where is the desk? It makes a set, you know, with the bookcase."

While the children hid their smiles and tried hard to look penitent, I explained to Queen Mary what had been done and why. She accepted the explanation, and said she understood.

"But," she said, "I hope that you had the desk labeled properly before it was put away."

Oh, yes; it had been labeled, and dated, and indexed, like everything else that had been stored away for future use. It is not only economy, but an active dislike of disorderliness that makes Queen Mary an outstanding example of thrift.

Nothing of hers is wasted. Every piece of knotted string, however intricate, is patiently unravelled, wound into a tidy bundle, usually by her own hands, and placed beside other tidy bundles in a drawer set aside for that special purpose. Every piece of creased wrapping paper is folded away for further use; every crumpled sheet of tissue paper gets the same care. We are all guilty of opening parcels and boxes with careless haste, eager to see the contents—but not Queen Mary: I have often watched her slitting the envelopes of her letters with graceful neatness and putting them in a basket ready to be re-sealed with wartime economy labels.

For many years Queen Mary has made a habit of collecting old Christmas cards from her relatives and close personal friends. These cards she uses for scrap-books, which delight the hearts of children in the hospitals of London. During times of public rejoicing, such as Princess Elizabeth's wedding, and the birth and christening of Prince Charles and Princess Anne, hundreds of beautiful cards arrive at Buckingham Palace from home and overseas. After being acknowledged they are put into what is known as "Queen Mary's Box."

With Queen Mary, tidiness of habit reveals tidiness of mind. Her desk itself shows how business-like her mind is. Everything is to hand; no energy is wasted in searching for anything that has got out of place, for everything is in its proper place.

Engagement book, address book, writing paper, envelopes, cards, memo-pads—everything is there, laid out with meticulous neatness, and there are little enamel boxes for smaller articles. Her pen-tray is silver. Also on her desk are many small photographs in gilt frames—a portrait gallery of her family and their children. One I shall always remember is a small snapshot of His Majesty, King George V, riding his dear old white pony in the grounds of Sandringham.

It could hardly have been from her mother, the Duchess of Teck, that Queen Mary inherited her methodical habits, her love of order, her sense of history and eagerness to learn. But she certainly did inherit her mother's sweet disposition and her capacity for friendship.

The Duchess of Teck was impulsive, warm-hearted, generous, and often unpredictable. She took frank and simple pleasure in the popularity she enjoyed, and she loved to be surrounded by entertaining, but not too clever, friends. She was not at all fond of Kensington Palace, the surroundings of which must have been less healthy than they are to-day. The Round Pond, which was overlooked by the nursery windows, had been neglected and was filthy, and when Princess May was fourteen months old she caught a chill which developed into an alarming illness. There was great anxiety for her, but soon she showed the strength of the constitution that was to stand all the stresses of her long life. As soon as the Princess was convalescent, the Duchess seized the excuse to move to the house of her own mother, the Duchess of Cambridge, at Kew, where the baby thrived.

Soon her mother wrote in a letter to a friend, "I short-coated her in the late Autumn, and she looked a perfect picture in her frocks and sashes." "Short-coating" was a ritual in those days. By that time the little Princess had a baby brother, Prince Adolphus ("Dolly"), who was followed by Prince Franz ("Frank," a remarkably handsome child), and Prince Alexander ("Alge").

People pointed out that the good looks of all the Teck children were inherited from the "dazzlingly lovely"

Countess Claudine Rhedey, who was killed by a fall from a horse when her son, the Duke of Teck, was a child. At the house of their other grandmother, the Duchess of Cambridge, at Kew, the Teck children were often shown her wonderful jewelry, including the famous emeralds that she had won in a Continental lottery.

There can have been no thought in anyone's mind that Princess May would ever wear those emeralds on her royal robes, as Queen of England. Unlike our own Princess Elizabeth, Queen Mary was not consciously brought up to be a Queen. Yet, reading between the lines of history, I think that she must have felt from the beginning that Fate was moving her in that course.

When she was very young, her parents were granted the use of the White Lodge in Richmond Park, where the Princess and her brothers enjoyed a much more expansive life than they could have had in the London of that day. There they often had as playmates "the Wales children," as the future King George V and his brothers were called. The Princess of Wales, the future Queen Alexandra, then at the height of her beauty, was often there and at Kensington Palace, where part of each winter was spent.

One little note from Alexandra to the Duchess of Teck is a treasure. "To-day," she wrote, "is Georgie's birthday. May your little girl come and play with him?"

Who could have guessed then that the "little girl" would one day be "Georgie's" bride?

At Richmond, the Teck children played cricket and picnicked in the woods; the boys learned to ride and shoot. But Mary, although she enjoyed fun as much as any, was less exuberant than the others. As she grew up she showed more and more her attachment to her mother, who gave her her first lessons, taught her to use the needle, read Scripture to her and heard her prayers. "Read psalms to May," says the Duchess in her diary. The children were taken sometimes to theaters, and they especially enjoyed pantomimes.

But when the Duchess thought there had been too many parties, she wrote to a friend: "A child has enough to do to learn obedience and attend to her lessons, and to grow, without too many parties and late hours. . . . There are too many grown-up children to-day."

Another entry in the Duchess's diary throws interesting light on Queen Mary's character as a girl: "At Lucy Kerr's I found Mamma and the others. May was shy at first and then wept, but finally recovered herself and played with the little girls. Home towards 7; May in tearing spirits all the way." Queen Mary was only three years old when that happened, but over and over again, as the Princess May grew up, her mother had occasion to remark on her shyness.

To-day that shyness is still there, but what an en-

Marion Crawford.

Woman's Own

The Duke and Duchess of Teck with
Princess Mary (in goat cart) and her
brothers, 1870.

Princess Victoria Agnes Augusta Mary
Louise Olga Pauline Claudine of Teck.

Queen Mary as a young woman.

Lafayette Ltd.

A special wedding day photograph of the Duke and Duchess of York, later George V and Queen Mary, 1893.

Queen Victoria with the Duke and
Duchess of York at Osborne after their
wedding.

Four Generations. King Edward VIII as a baby.

Picture Post

Queen Mary and King George V (when
Prince and Princess of Wales) with Edward
VIII.

Queen Mary and King George VI.

Queen Victoria presides over a Royal Family party at Osborne House in 1898.

Picture Post

The Duke and Duchess of York with
their children at Abergeldie.

King George V and Queen Mary at
Cowes with the Prince of Wales, 1908.

Queen Mary in a colliery tram during a visit to a Merthyr colliery in 1912.

P.A.-Reuter.

The great Victory March, 1919. The King and Queen, with the Queen

Queen Mary with Princess Mary (in
V.A.D. uniform) at Buckingham Palace,
1919.

British Information Ser

Queen Mary with King George V at the
Marathon Race at Windsor in 1919.

dearing quality it has become! Perhaps, in a way, it was because the Duchess was expansive and animated in conversation and the Princess was so reserved and retiring that conversation with strangers was often a painful ordeal to her. Some people said that Mary could never learn to make small talk because she was awed to silence by her mother's conversational brilliance. Similarly, as the Duchess was careless about hours of appointments, Mary became a model of punctuality.

Until she was well into her teens, Princess May showed little sign that she was on her way to become one of the best informed and most highly educated of all the royal personages of her time. Perhaps the first person to discover in her something more than normal intelligence was her Alsatian governess, Madame Bricka, who, coming to White Lodge when Princess May was sixteen, was delighted to find her eager to learn everything that was to be learned. The Princess showed that she wanted much more than a training in the "ladylike" accomplishments and graces that would have been enough to carry her through the duties of a leader of society.

People who remember Madame Bricka tell me that she herself was highly educated, liberal in outlook, and remarkable for her strength of character and devotion to her pupil. She made such an impression on Princess May that years later when her son Edward, the young Prince of Wales, needed his first lessons, Madame

Bricka was made his teacher. And she remained a life-long friend of Queen Mary.

I have heard Queen Mary called self-educated. I should say rather that her education was self-imposed. She so obviously chose her own way and knew where she was going. And she deliberately chose the hard way. She plied Bricka with questions on every subject under the sun, and kept Bricka searching until she had the answers. May must have been the sort of pupil that every conscientious teacher dreams of.

When a foreign poet, musician, artist, or writer was coming to the White Lodge, it was Bricka's task to dig up all the information she could about the visitor, his work and his country. The Princess may have been too shy to make small talk, but it seemed most important to her that she should have good knowledge of the lives and work of distinguished people whom she met. She admired people who could do things, and she still does.

Later she was to amaze other members of the Royal Family, and especially her husband, King George V, with her knowledge of people, places and problems. "I don't know how May does it," said King George more than once when, on official visits, she showed herself able to discuss with experts the places and things she and the King had come to inspect.

Some royal visits may be taken as graceful gestures of interest and good will, but to Queen Mary they have always meant much more. On one such occasion, an official heard her asking the experts question after question. "Does all this really mean anything to her?" he asked her lady-in-waiting. "Mean anything!" she replied. "The Queen will go straight home and read everything she can find on the subject."

All that explains what I mean when I say that Queen Mary could have been brilliantly successful in any career that she chose for herself. But, born a Princess, she resigned herself to her destiny and chose the path of duty. That path was already becoming clear to her when, at the age of sixteen, she suddenly found her manner of living drastically changed.

Her parents, the Duke and Duchess, had to move from Kensington Palace and White Lodge because they simply could not afford to live there in the style that was expected of them. For several years they had been forced to spend more money than was coming in.

Some people have said that the Duchess was extravagant, but I think it would be fairer to call her over-generous. As Princess Mary of Cambridge, she had been brought up to believe that she was called upon to keep up a high standard of living in her household and she had not been taught to be a good manager. It was not so much that she spent a great deal on her personal needs as that she had most generous notions of hospitality. No messenger ever came to her house without being given a meal. She had to have carriages and horses, had to subscribe to many charities and had to entertain largely.

All that came to an end when a royal hint was dropped that it would be better for everyone if the Teck family went abroad for a while. Such a hint was a command.

So the Duke and Duchess, with Princess May and her brothers, soon found themselves whisked from the royal state of Kensington and Richmond to the second floor of a private hotel on the Lung-Arno at Florence.

To the Princess May's parents, that must have been something like exile, but the Duchess's sense of humor overrode other feelings. When she and her family went to stay with relatives in Switzerland, Prince Francis, May's brother, wrote to a friend:

"We are living in three separate little houses—Papa, Dolly, I and Baby in one, Mamma and May in another, and in the third, cousin William of Würtemberg lives with his little girl."

This uprooting of the family was the first great turning point in Queen Mary's life—if it is possible to speak of turning points in a career that was always to be so steadfastly pursued.

Certainly the change was a shock at first to the shy, sensitive girl. She was homesick. Italian ways were strange to her, and beautiful Florence was not at its best when they arrived in mid-October. The famed River Arno, "very narrow and poor and quite brown," was a poor exchange for the lordly Thames. Watching a review in honor of the Italian King's birthday, she thought the cavalry were "awful;" compared the troops unfavorably with the Guards at home, and wished she were watching the Trooping of the Colour from "Uncle George's window at the Horse Guards."

It was little consolation to her that foreign Royalties and other visitors trooped into Florence from all parts of Europe to see the "English Royalties."

At the British Consulate she attended her first "grown-up" ball, and also, that first winter, she found private theatricals at the Palazzo Renuccini "quite amusing" and the flower show in the Cascine (so far from Chelsea!) "great fun." But soon she was to see that the stay abroad was opening to her freedom of a new and wonderful kind, and a god-sent opportunity to prepare her mind and body for whatever work the future held for her. And we know from her own letter to me, how Queen Mary felt about all that when she was seventeen.

PART FOUR

IT was always a wonderful experience, and a great privilege, for me to ride in Queen Mary's motor-car when she went about London with the Princesses on the Monday outings.

Although on such drives there is no ceremony, and the Royal car takes its place in traffic with the rest, Queen Mary knows that she will be recognized and she always sits upright on one of the small seats in the middle of the car, in order that she may see and be seen.

She is greatly interested in all she sees, and especially in people. As she goes along, she frequently comments in a very characteristic way.

Once, for example, when the car was slowed down in a busy street, she saw across the pavement a man carrying something heavy, and she said as if to herself:

"Now, where do you think that man is going with that picture?" I am sure she would have liked to stop and ask him, for pictures are almost a passion with Queen Mary. But he did not realize who was looking at him so interestedly, and he went on his way and soon was lost to sight.

"What a pretty girl!" I once heard her exclaim. It was raining hard, and the girl who had caught Queen Mary's eye was enveloped in a transparent raincoat. Her hood, covered an amusing little hat like a garden of flowers, but left open to the rain a truly lovely, radiant face, smiling as if she enjoyed the downpour. She could not have looked happier if she had actually heard the queenly words of approval.

People who step off the pavement in the way of traffic fill Queen Mary with anxiety for their safety. "Silly man!" I heard her say. "Why does he try to cross there, when there is a perfectly safe crossing a few yards away?"

She always acknowledges, with a gracious bow, the salutes of those who recognize her. The look of pleased surprise on some of their faces must be familiar to her, and it has never failed to thrill me.

Sometimes, having acknowledged a salute from the occupants of a car, Queen Mary is amused, on stopping at the next traffic light, to find that the car has hurried to be there at the same time; and then the greetings are graciously repeated.

The faces of some of the people on her regular routes have long been well-known to her, and she can always pick them out. Mostly they are old ladies and gentlemen who have known for years just where to wait. They look for her, and she looks for them, and they know that the smile she gives them is really their own.

And it is not only in London that Queen Mary can go about happily, untroubled by fuss or crowds. There can be few towns in this country that she has not visited at one time or another. I do not mean on official visits, for opening new buildings, laying foundation stones, and such public functions, but on brief, quiet unofficial visits —to call on friends, to see an ancient building or some other monument of historic interest, or to search the antique shops for objects of art and craftsmanship.

Naturally, she has had more opportunity in later years for such private visits than in the years when she shared the throne and was constantly engaged in official duties, and she has made good use of her freedom, even in war-time. The word goes round: "Do you know that Queen Mary was in . . . to-day?" Her car has been seen in the High Street; and someone is bound to know someone who knows someone who actually saw her step into or out of it. In a little while the whole town knows, but by then the royal visit is over.

It is almost an unwritten law that no mention is made in the local newspapers of such unofficial comings and goings. Those whom she has occasion to meet are always discreet, respecting her right to as much privacy as possible. And people in the streets who catch sight of Queen Mary show their high regard for her by not crowding about her. Indeed, they behave just as well as if they were guests at a royal garden party. The British people as a whole are like that.

Although Queen Mary spends less time nowadays than she used to in acquiring new pieces for her collections, museums, antique shops and curiosity shops, often in quite out-of-the-way places, have always been favorite hunting grounds of Queen Mary.

"It is downright uncanny," said an antique dealer to me one day, after she had spent half an hour in inspecting his stock and was ready to go. What constantly amazed him at every visit was not so much her evident familiarity with the whole field of antiques, from Georgian furniture to Oriental ceramics, as the skill with which she went straight to the objects she wanted most to examine, only glancing casually at the showpieces that were set out to catch the customers' eyes.

"She seems to know," he said, "not only just what she wants, but exactly where to look for it. Having found it, she can tell me more about its history, associations and value than I know myself."

Everything she owns, acquires, gives away or lends for exhibition, has a history and a meaning. Age alone, or even rarity, is not enough to commend a thing to her. Antiques represent only one phase of her many interests, but they are important because they appeal to that strong historical sense which has always inspired her.

That sense began to show itself when she was still a girl, the constant playmate of her young cousins, the children of Edward, Prince of Wales, and Princess Alexandra. Even then her quiet reserve and studious ways seemed to indicate that she had more than an inkling of her own high destiny.

From her mother she first learned to open her eyes to the beauties of good craftsmanship, for the Duchess had an expert knowledge of antiques, especially of English period furniture. But it was of her own accord that the young Princess discovered what an opportunity had been put in her way when, for the sake of economy, she, her parents, and her brothers, left London to live in Florence.

For the Duchess, accustomed until then to large-scale entertaining and plenty of money to spend, life in Florence must have seemed like exile, at least at first.

But soon she was the center of social life, with a stream of visitors from the courts of Europe coming to see the "English Royalties," and the Duchess became quite at home in the little Italian city. Not so Princess May, until she discovered what a treasure-house of art and beauty and historical associations Florence really was.

Then she threw off her home-sickness and began to explore the art galleries, churches and palaces, finding something new every day, and taking careful note of all she saw. She visited studios and watched sculptors and painters at work. Honored, they were delighted to answer her questions, and she was an eager listener. The wonders she saw about her filled in the background of dates and facts that she had been given in the schoolroom.

Visits to the house where the poet Dante lived, and the church where he was married, fired her imagination and set her reading the great works of Italian and French writers, filling in the gaps of her reading, making up for lost time.

People who wonder nowadays how Queen Mary can find the energy to go on walking for hours at exhibitions, museums and flower shows, or through hospital wards or over housing estates, keeping alert and interested when others are tired out, may find one explanation in her early self-training. Before she was eighteen she had acquired the appetite for sightseeing, and was never happier than when she was going through galleries and palaces with her notebook in her hand, studying painting and sculpture.

She seemed to feel that she might never again have such an opportunity as those two years in Italy gave her, and she used every hour of it, not only indoors, but also tramping the countryside to see ancient ruins and historic churches, studying history in the places where it had been made. Already she was beginning to prepare herself to play the great part in history to which, although she did not know it yet, she was to be called.

When she returned to England, after visiting Venice and Paris, she went to live with her parents in a house which had been lent to them in Chester Square, London.

The great Sarah Bernhardt once described Chester Square as "a small square of somber green, with a black statue in the middle and an ugly church," but surely it was never quite so gloomy as that and, if it had been, the Duchess of Teck would soon have brightened it up.

A round of entertainments, including the first dinner and dance in Princess May's honor, had been arranged when suddenly a stop was put to all gaiety by the death of her grandfather, Duke Paul of Würtemberg. So for two months of that summer the Princess had to wear black instead of gay summer frocks. No wonder she still dislikes black, considering how often as a girl she had to wear mourning!

But she wore white, of course, for her Confirmation, which was administered by the Bishop of St. Albans in the Chapel Royal, Windsor; and a little later, in a pale blue gauze dress that set off her young charms to perfection, she was presented at court.

Because she was technically within the succession to the throne, she did not have to "pass" Queen Victoria with the other debutantes, but was "presented in the Closet"—making her curtsy and receiving Queen Victoria's kiss of welcome in the small apartment from which the Queen emerged into the Throne Room.

And then the public life of Princess May began, with a constant round of engagements to encroach on the program of study and needlework that she had laid out for herself at White Lodge, Richmond Park, where her parents had returned to live.

At dances, although she was the junior of all the Princesses, she could not be asked to dance, but had to "send for" her partners, according to the rigid etiquette of the Court. She had to sit through stiff, formal dinners and listen to long speeches; and there was hardly a day without a bazaar to open, a parish hall to inspect, a prize-giving or a charity concert to attend.

To carry out these duties, she had to overcome her shyness as best she could. At first it was an ordeal for her to appear before an audience and talk with officials, but even then she was taking note of all she saw and heard, and recording each day's events in her diary.

All through her long life, Queen Mary has set down each day's events in her diary. It is a habit that she learned as a child from her mother. To this day, when she comes back to Marlborough House from a public function, or even from a private visit, her hat is hardly off before she is making notes and memoranda, to be transcribed just before she goes to bed, in the book of hand-tooled leather, with a lock and key, which she keeps in her bedroom. There is a whole page for each day's doings, and so, through the years, she must have written hundreds of thousands of words—the whole story of an era, by one who has played a noble part in it.

These writings are unique; no other Royal personage has ever kept so complete a record. It will be of untold value to future generations, but it has been of immediate value also to Queen Mary, enabling her to refresh her memory. When she is going to visit a city, there is no need for her to ask a secretary to remind her whom she had met and what she did last time she was there. Even if her remarkable memory hesitated, she could turn at once to her own written record.

"Keep up your diary, my dear," said Queen Mary to Princess Elizabeth as soon as the little Princess could read and write. "Write in it every day. You will never regret it." And she gave both Princess Elizabeth and Princess Margaret diaries, bound in leather like her own. These diaries were kept on their bedside tables, and every night at bedtime I asked them whether they had written down the day's events. Sometimes, when they were very young, the task took them a long time, and so it often did later, when they had a lot to write about.

I have told in the story of "The Little Princesses" of Princess Elizabeth's long ordeal on the day of the funeral of her grandfather, King George V—how she and I reached Paddington Station an hour too soon, how she waited, white-faced, among the silent, often weeping people, how she watched the procession, with the gun-carriage covered with the Union Jack and heard the bands playing the Dead March, and how, when it was all over, she joined her parents on the platform and went with them to Windsor.

That night, before Princess Elizabeth went to bed, I asked her whether she had written up her diary. She had, she said; and I wondered how she had set down the story of that long, sad day in so short a time. In silent sorrow she let me glance at what she had written. Two words only—"Grandpapa's funeral." That was all she had been able to bring herself to write.

One of the last sad duties that Queen Mary was able to do for her husband when he lay dying at Sandringham was to make the last entry in his own leather-bound diary.

He had tried, but some of the words were barely decipherable. References to snow and wind could be made out, and the name of his physician-in-ordinary, Lord Dawson of Penn, but no more. Then, in Queen Mary's handwriting, this note was added:

My dearest husband, King Geo. V was much distressed at the bad handwriting above and begged me to write his diary for him the next day. He passed away on January 20th at 5 minutes before midnight.

Mary R.

When I learned of that, I remembered the first words King George V ever spoke to me, when I met him with Queen Mary on the lawn at the Royal Lodge, Windsor, at the very beginning of my service as governess to the

Little Princesses: "For goodness sake, teach Margaret and Lilibet to write a decent hand." As for Queen Mary, she has always taken care to write every word as if she knew that posterity would want to read it, and as if she wanted to save posterity trouble.

Queen Mary, as Princess May, was twenty years old at the time of Queen Victoria's Golden Jubilee, in 1887. This was the first great public celebration in which Queen Victoria had taken part since the death of the Prince Consort twenty-five years before.

Even at the wedding of her son, the future King Edward VII, to Princess Alexandra she had sat apart in the Royal pew at St. George's Chapel, Windsor, and had seen nothing of the festivity and rejoicing. But for the Golden Jubilee she did come out to make a State progress to a Thanksgiving Service in Westminster Abbey.

"The gorgeousness of the surroundings," says a chronicler, "threw into sharper contrast the little figure dressed in plain black, looking perhaps the smaller because she chose to sit with no one beside herself.

"Facing her in the carriage, drawn by the famous 'Creams,' sat Alexandra, Princess of Wales, and the then Crown Princess of Prussia, while there rode ahead a cortege of Princes of her own House. In the other carriages were to be seen the Queen's other daughters and daughters-in-law, the junior members of the family 'proceeding privately' to the Abbey Church.

"Thus it came about that on a great historic occasion three Princesses destined to be the Consorts of the rulers of Russia, Rumania, and Great Britain passed unobserved to take their places in the Abbey, although all along the route the crowds had given a great ovation to the beaming Duchess of Teck and her fair daughter."

Few then could have guessed that Princess May, the fair daughter, would ride as Queen of England, in the Royal State Coach—four tons of gilt and gold, that King George III had built at a cost of £7,500. That coach, which served in seven reigns, has not been seen in the streets of London since King George VI rode in it to open Parliament in 1938. It was laid up in the Royal Mews during the Second World War. Now it is being renovated, with brakes and rubber tires instead of iron, and soon it will figure in Royal processions again, probably with Windsor Greys instead of the famous "Creams" drawing it.

It was in connection with Jubilee functions, Jubilee presentations and Jubilee memorials that Princess May began to show that close interest in the life and welfare of ordinary people, and especially working people, that she has shown all her life. For a Children's Jubilee Offering, the Princess, making the first of her rare personal appeals, collected £200.

Just at that time the House of Lords had appointed a Select Committee to inquire into the sweatshops of the East End of London. Princess May, who then had set herself a course of reading that took up six hours every day, on top of her social engagements, met Lord Dunraven at the White Lodge one day and staggered him by asking where she could learn the whole truth about the way poor people lived and worked.

It was something new, and it even seemed rather shocking, for a Princess to be interested in such things except in a loftily, charitable way. She sent for the Blue Book on "sweating" and then for other official publications, and she set herself to work at them with the same energy that she had given to art and literature.

She must even then have longed for the time when she could go into the factories and see the people at work, and then into their homes, to see how they lived. She had to learn from official reports of the low wages that were then being paid to women workers in the "needle trades," and she was horrified by what she read. She horrified Court dressmakers by asking them questions about conditions under which the embroidery was done. A Princess was not supposed to bother her head with such things, but this Princess did.

The time was coming when she would take tea with miners' wives in South Wales coal villages, and visit the industrial plants of Yorkshire, the railway works at Crewe and the potteries of Staffordshire, and see what no Queen had ever seen before. We may be sure that all this has been set down in her diaries.

There is a little verse, not good as poetry, but full of

meaning, that Princess May learned at the time when her heart was first touched by the plight of women workers in certain trades:

> If each man in his measure
> Would do a brother's part
> To cast a ray of sunlight
> Into a brother's heart,
> How changed would be our country;
> How changed would be our poor,
> And then might Merrie England
> Deserve her name once more.

One of Queen Mary's most cherished possessions is a jeweled fan of exquisite workmanship that formerly belonged to her beloved grandmother, the Duchess of Cambridge, who died at the age of ninety-two, when Princess May was in her twenty-second year.

Although that remarkable old lady was crippled by paralysis for her last fifteen years, her brain was crystal-clear. She had vivid memories of King George III, the death of Nelson at Trafalgar, and the gaieties of the Regency period, and she often talked about them to Princess May, who always had a special place in her grandmother's heart.

To-day I often think how wonderful it is that little Prince Charles and Princess Anne, when they grow up, will be able to say that their grandmother, Queen Mary, heard of the events of two centuries before from one who had lived through them. What a strong link between the past and the future Queen Mary is!

There was something curiously prophetic about the bequest of that jeweled fan to Princess May, for her grandmother specifically stated in her will that it was to be "a wedding present." The Duchess of Cambridge must have had more than an inkling of the brilliant future that was in store for the Princess.

In the two years following the death of her grandmother, Princess May went to Oberammergau to see the Passion Play, to the Italian Lakes, and to some of the continental art galleries, and she had shared in the festivities that marked the Silver Wedding anniversary of her parents. They had been married in Kew Church, and the Princess and her three brothers attended the anniversary service there. There were garden parties at Kew and Richmond, and a brilliant season was crowned in the following winter by the announcement that Princess May was to be married to the Duke of Clarence, "Prince Eddy," eldest son of Edward and Alexandra, and heir-presumptive to the throne.

By this time the British people had taken Princess May so much to their hearts that they welcomed with joy the news that she was to be the bride of the heir-presumptive to the throne.

Prince Eddy, although amiable, gifted and a popular figure—"sweet-natured," they called him—was quiet and reserved. He bore a striking resemblance to his beautiful mother. He and his brother George, the future King, were, as children, inseparable playmates. They served together as naval cadets in the training ship *Britannia*, taking their full share of the hard life of the ship, living mostly on salt pork and ship's biscuits.

The commander of the *Britannia*, Commander Hill, afterwards wrote about Prince George:

"I want you to realise that when he joined up he was only about 12½ years old, and that he actually went to sea at 14½. Yet, even at this early age he had, when in charge of one of the ship's cutters, for instance, to accept full responsibility for the lives of men. He also had to endure all the discomforts and all the hardships which were the inevitable and common lot of anyone who went to sea in those days.

"In my humble opinion the training he thus obtained in the Royal Navy, and the strict discipline to which he was subject, were tremendous factors in forming the character of the great and lovable man and wise king he afterwards became."

Prince Eddy left the sea soon after completing his training, but Prince George stayed in the service, and was still very much "the Sailor Prince."

But just then, at the end of a spell ashore, Prince George came down with an attack of typhoid fever, which caused great anxiety and kept him in bed for six weeks. It was while he was still very ill that he learned that Prince Eddy and Princess May had become engaged during a houseparty at Luton Hoo, given by the Danish Minister and Mme. de Falbe.

That was on December 3rd, 1891, when Prince George was twenty-six years old. He had hardly recovered from his illness, and weighed only a little more than 130 pounds, when influenza broke out in the family. His younger sister, Princess Victoria, was the first to fall ill, and next Prince Eddy. The influenza must have been of the same virulent type that wrought such havoc in all parts of the world at the end of the First World War, for it ran a rapid course.

On January 8th, the eve of Prince Eddy's twenty-eighth birthday, he took to his bed. After a day or two, inflammation of the lungs set in. On January 13th, he was delirious and sinking rapidly. All that night his parents sat by his bedside, Princess Alexandra bathing his forehead. Early the next morning all the members of the family were summoned to his bedside, and at half-past nine he died—less than six weeks after his engagement to Princess May. He was buried in the Memorial Chapel at Windsor. Prince George was still too weak to walk in the sad procession.

Older people vividly remember the shock with which they heard the news.

I have often heard them speak of those anxious days, and especially of the sympathy that was extended to Princess May by all sorts and conditions of men and women. Prince George wrote in his journals of his grief at the loss of his beloved brother and close companion, and he wrote also of the courage and resignation of Princess May, the most tragic figure of the swift, sorrowful drama.

For more than a year, Princess May removed herself from the public eye. She spent a few months at Richmond, and then her mother took her to Eastbourne and to France. To France also went the stunned and broken Prince and Princess of Wales and their family. Meanwhile, after a setback, with many sleepless nights, caused by the shock of his brother's death, Prince George's health improved rapidly.

"To me," wrote Prince George to a shipmate, "his loss is irreparable, as you know how devoted we always were. We had never been separated until I was eighteen. . . . The whole of my life is changed." Indeed it was, in a double sense, for now he was the heir-presumptive, with a new line of duties and responsibilities before him.

In May, he was well enough to go to Denmark for the Golden Wedding anniversary of his Danish grandparents. It was while he was there that Queen Victoria headed her Birthday Honors List by the announcement that she had created him Duke of York. It was an ancient and illustrious title, but for some reason known to herself, Queen Victoria disliked it. "The Queen," she wrote in a footnote to a memorandum, "does not at all wish to revive the title of York, or she would have

done so for her own son Alfred." In the memorandum,
her secretary had set out a list of titles suitable for the
Prince of Wales' sons. Before being persuaded to change
her mind about Prince George's new title, she proposed
that he be called Duke of London. But the title of York,
and the man and woman who bore it, were soon to become beloved everywhere.

The Duke took his seat, with due ceremony, in the
House of Lords. Plans were put in hand for preparing
the cottage at Sandringham (soon to be called York
Cottage) and certain rooms in St. James's Palace were
readied for his use.

And then the Sailor Prince went back to sea for
strenuous manœuvres in which he commanded the
Melampus for months of heavy, unseasonable weather.
Later, at Christmas time, he visited Queen Victoria at
Windsor, where she spoke to him long and earnestly
about his future. He was nearly twenty-eight years old.
Had he thought of marriage? He had.

We know from the old Queen's letters and diaries
what a warm place Prince George held in her heart. She
confided in him more freely than in any other relative,
even the Prince of Wales. The letters she wrote to him
during the eighteen months following the death of
Prince Eddy show her devoted affection for him, her
appreciation of his high character, and her confidence
in his future.

It is known now that she had set her heart on his

marriage to the Princess May. That was what she spoke to him about at Windsor, and returned to in her letters, which he received at Sandringham, on the Royal Yacht *Osborne* during a Mediterranean cruise in the Spring of 1892 and in Rome, where he represented the Queen at the Silver Wedding celebrations of the King and Queen of Italy.

It was during the Prince's absence abroad that Mr. Gladstone, the Prime Minister, sought an audience of Queen Victoria and expressed the popular—he might almost have said clamorous—desire that the Duke of York should marry Princess May. If such a marriage could be arranged, said Mr. Gladstone, it would give great and lasting satisfaction.

Queen Victoria's reply is not recorded, but that could easily have been one of the occasions when she *was* amused. She was never very fond of Mr. Gladstone, so perhaps she said to him, "Too late, as usual, Mr. Prime Minister." For on Prince George's return to London, at the end of April, he had gone straight to East Sheen Lodge, to stay with his sister, the Duchess of Fife.

Another guest at the Lodge was Princess May. On the afternoon of Wednesday, May 3rd, he walked with her in the garden, told her what was in his heart, and heard the words he had longed to hear. He wrote:

"The darling girl consented to be my wife. I am so happy."

PART FIVE

SITTING with my husband in the Poets' Corner of Westminster Abbey at the wedding of Princess Elizabeth, I found myself thinking of the calm, thoughtful face of Queen Mary, who had already taken her seat with the other members of the Royal Family. What a pageant of history must have been passing before her mind's eye! Perhaps she was thinking of other royal weddings she had known—of her daughter's, of her sons', and of Princess Ena's in Madrid long ago, when a bomb had been thrown at the royal carriage. But surely the most vivid picture in her mind was that of her own marriage to Prince George, Duke of York, in the Chapel Royal, on July 6th, 1893.

We know what another Queen, Victoria, was thinking on that day, long ago. Victoria too had looked down the arches of the years. "I could not but remember," she wrote, "that I had stood where May did, fifty-three years ago, and dear Vicky thirty-five years ago, and that the dear ones, who stood where Georgie did, were gone from us. May these dear children's happiness last longer!"

Now Queen Mary has lived even longer and much more actively than Queen Victoria, and her vision of history is even wider than Victoria's. She has lived to see Victoria's prayer answered in the happiness of her children's children.

The wedding of Princess May to the Duke of York took place three months after he had proposed to her in the garden of East Sheen Lodge, the home of his sister, the Duchess of Fife. They were busy months, with Royal personages arriving from Russia, Germany, Belgium and Denmark. Public enthusiasm was high and the excitement intense, not only because the couple were exceedingly popular, but also because the bride-to-be was the first British Princess to marry a future King of England for more than 300 years.

"The felicitations offered to the Duke of York," said the *Morning Post* newspaper, "will be both spontaneous and sincere. He is fortunately able to please both himself, and to delight the nation at the same time by the choice of a Princess whose name has a sympathetic charm for all, and whose future will be followed by all with constant interest. She is essentially a daughter of England. As a great-granddaughter of George III, she stands in the line of succession to the throne. More, not only by birth, but by education and domicile, she belongs to England. She possesses every qualification for the high place that awaits her."

The sailor Prince and the English Princess! No wonder great crowds cheered them on their almost daily appearances, driving in Hyde Park or to the Opera.

The Duke visited the Princess at White Lodge in Richmond Park, and she went with her parents, the Duke and Duchess of Teck, to visit him at Marlborough House. Meanwhile their future home, York Castle at Sandringham, was being made ready, and the Duke went there to inspect the work. He also found time to see "Isinglass" win the Derby, and to go to Ascot from London each day of the meeting. Then he returned to Sandringham where, only a few days before his wedding day, he came down with a bad attack of neuralgia, and had to rest.

The bride-to-be was even busier. More than 1,500 presents, valued at £300,000, poured in, and all had to be set out for the great day. Hundreds of letters arrived daily and, knowing Queen Mary, we may be sure that they were acknowledged promptly.

Bells were rung, flags were flown and cannon were fired at Richmond when Princess May, at a garden party there, said farewell to friends and neighbors whom she had known all her life. Neighbours from Kew presented an address to her at Cambridge House, and her reply was addressed to "my old friends at Kew."

I have often heard it said that Queen Mary never makes a speech. Certainly she made one that day, and it is on record. "It is with sincere pleasure," said the Princess, "that I have listened to the words which have just been read, and I wish to say that I thank you most truly and very deeply for the congratulations that you have offered to me. The reference that you have made to my dear grandmother and mother, as also to other members of my family, and to the early years of my life, in great measure passed among you, has touched me much. And I can assure you that I shall always remember this occasion and the kindness shown to me by old friends at Kew, to whom I beg you to convey my warm thanks for their good wishes."

Also on record is this, from the people of Kew and Richmond: "We loved her for her own sake and for the sake of the dear, warm-hearted mother, the idol of everyone, high and low, whose sympathy knew no bounds." And they remembered that they had "watched her grow up to womanhood, always with the silent hope that some day she may be our Queen."

So she said farewell to the happy scenes of her girlhood—the garden and lawn where she had enjoyed so many parties, the Church in Kingston Vale where she had worshipped, the lanes where she had walked.

Princess May chose as her bridesmaids a bevy of Princesses—the Princesses Victoria and Maud of Wales, the

daughters of the Duke of Edinburgh (excepting Queen
Marie of Roumania), the daughters of the Duke of Connaught, Princess Helena Victoria, Princess Ena of Battenberg (the future Queen of Spain), and Princess Alice
of Battenberg. It was probably the first and last Royal
Wedding when so many Princesses were bridesmaids,
for it had been the custom until then for daughters of
great peers to be chosen.

What excitement there must have been at White
Lodge while Princess May's wedding clothes were being designed and made! It is easy for me to picture the
scene, for I have watched Queen Mary in Marlborough
House working on one of the many panels of the wonderful carpet which she made for sale in the United
States to help the drive for dollars.

It is an entrancing sight to see her regally upright
figure, sitting at her embroidery, with the many-colored silks and wools in her workbasket. She had her
first lessons in sewing and embroidery from her mother
at White Lodge, and she hoped that Princess Elizabeth
would do the same. But, alas, Princess Elizabeth has not
a natural gift for it. At the age of eight she managed,
with great pains, and with encouragement from me, to
produce a small linen tray-cloth for "Grannie," who was
greatly pleased. It was beige, with a border of weave
stitch in red. After that, Princess Elizabeth confined her
efforts to making blotters for Queen Mary's birthday
presents. She was happier at measuring and cutting

cardboard than using a needle. Queen Mary was particularly delighted and wrote to me to say so, when in later years Princess Elizabeth managed to get her Girl Guide Badge for sewing.

Queen Mary as a girl could have won badges by the score, and not only for needlework. Even before her marriage she had been a member of the Royal School of Needlework, and even now she never misses an exhibition of the school's work at South Kensington. Her own work, particularly the *gros point* in wool for which she is famous, has often been shown at exhibitions of the Embroiderers' Guild. Her expert advice is often sought when altar cloths, vestments and valuable pieces of lace and embroidery are sent to the Royal School of Needlework for repair.

And of course there is Queen Mary's Needlework Guild, which, from small beginnings (when Queen Mary, as Duchess of York, took it over from Lady Wolverton fifty-three years ago) now has branches all over the world.

The original purpose of the Guild was to collect blankets, clothing and other necessities for poor people, and to sew for them. Since then its scope has grown enormously. During the war, the Guild sent hundreds of thousands of gifts of clothing and other articles to bombed-out people. Once the Guild received a large contribution which some of the members wondered whether it was advisable to accept.

"Certainly," said Queen Mary. "No one should be prevented from doing a good action. No kindly impulse will ever be checked by me, no matter where it springs from."

That also was an echo from her girlhood days, when it was said that no deserving person was ever turned away from her mother's door. And "deserving" meant anyone who did the family a service, even if it was only delivering a message or the milk.

So we can easily imagine that the choosing and making of her wedding clothes was an enjoyable and absorbing task to the young Princess who was one day to become Queen Mary. She was already an expert on materials as well as handiwork, and since reading about the conditions in the textile trades, was quite likely to ask questions about seamstresses' wages and hours of work.

One stipulation she made was that everything in the trousseau was to be of British manufacture—"all the silk from England, all the flannel from Wales, all the tweed from Scotland, and every yard of lace and poplin from Ireland."

Princess May was already noted for the simple elegance of her gowns, although what was called simple then would be elaborate to-day. In her teens, she had gone to Court in a wasp-waisted gown, made from twenty-five yards of satin and tulle, frilled and ruched, with full bustle and long train. Her wedding dress was of white satin, with a silver design of roses, shamrocks and thistles interwoven.

At Queen Victoria's invitation, Princess May and her mother stayed at Buckingham Palace for two nights before the wedding, and her mother was invited, as a great privilege, to drive with the Queen to the Chapel in the "new glass coach."

It is, of course, no miracle, but nevertheless it is a remarkable historical fact that the sun usually shines on our royal brides. We expect it, and generally it happens. For Princess Elizabeth, the sun broke through the clouds on an unpromising November morning. For her parents, in 1923, the April day dawned dull and wet, but, as King George V wrote in his diary, "the sun actually came out as the bride entered the Abbey."

No happy couple could have wished for more glorious weather than Princess May and Prince George had on their wedding day.

In the morning, when the Princess, wearing her bridal gown, went into the Queen's room, Victoria (says Edith Sitwell), "felt as if the sky were made of blue flowers, forget-me-nots, and speedwells, and the bride's eyes were a deeper heaven."

Later in the day Queen Victoria was to complain that the weather was "overpoweringly hot." That was after she had arrived at the Chapel Royal ahead of time, through a misunderstanding, and had been received by an embarrassed usher instead of by an important Officer of State. But the Queen only smiled; it was a happy day for her, and for everyone else.

London, with the streets hung with roses and may-blossoms, looked like one great flower garden. The bridegroom, with his father, the Prince of Wales, and his uncle, the Duke of Connaught, drove to St. James's Palace via Piccadilly and St. James's Street.

"At 12.30," he wrote in his diary, "darling May and I were married in the Chapel Royal by the Archbishop. I am indeed lucky to have got such a charming and darling wife."

And here is Queen Victoria's story of the wedding: "The Queen of Denmark came in with her grandson the Cesarewitch, and dear Alix (looking very pale) with her father. The bridegroom's procession followed rapidly, he being supported by his father and Uncle Affie, all in naval uniform.

"They had to wait a short time, when the bride appeared, followed by her ten dear bridesmaids, Victoria, Maud, Ducky, Sandra, Baby B., Thora, Daisy, Patsy, Alice Battenberg and Ena, the four little ones looking very sweet.

"George gave his answers very distinctly, while May, quite self-possessed, spoke very low."

Then, in the Palace, there was a great luncheon party, where the visiting Royalties were as gay as any of the guests. Group photographs were taken, and that was a much longer process than modern cameras would have made it. Crowds surged in the Mall, and Queen Victoria appeared on the balcony to present the happy pair to them.

At 4.30 the new Duchess of York, "looking sweet and young in her dress of white poplin edged with gold, and her pretty little toque with roses," said good-bye to everyone and drove away with her husband in an open carriage with an escort of The Blues, through cheering crowds to Liverpool Street Station to take the train for Sandringham.

The Duke in a black frock coat, the Duchess in her delicate white dress, drove in an open carriage from Wolferton station along the dusty road to York Cottage, the little house that the Prince of Wales had given his son. The feet of the horses churned up the dust. When the couple arrived at the threshold of their new home the Duke seemed to be in white, the Duchess in black. But they were too tired and happy to notice.

One of the first things the Duchess unpacked was a small china ornament, with the figures of a boy and girl, kissing. It had cost only a few pence in a bazaar, but it was precious; for it had come to her, "with love from Georgie," years before, when she was a little girl.

Many of those happy scenes of long ago must have passed before Queen Mary's mind on the day of Princess Elizabeth's wedding. I do not think that my admiration for her was ever greater than at that time, when she seemed to me, as indeed she was, a living bridge between the past and the future.

Looking back only a few years, I found it difficult to realize that the little girl whom I had first seen sitting up on her bed, with reins on her bedpost, "driving her horses in Windsor Great Park," had grown up to be the radiant Princess walking down the aisle on the arm of her handsome husband, Prince Philip.

As for Queen Mary, only she can know what that vision of youth meant to her. Like myself, she was losing a little of something she loved.

I remember that later on that grey November day when the Princess left Buckingham Palace with her husband, I did not run to the outer gates as most of the wedding guests did, to catch a last glimpse of the happy couple. Instead, I stood in the Grand Hall and watched the carriage go out under the arch to the forecourt. As I stood there, feeling very sad, with rose petals all around my feet, Queen Mary came and stood beside me. She kissed my cheek, pressed my arm and said: "Lilibet is so happy, and to-day has been wonderful." The Queen of Holland, then Princess Juliana, joined us and said how proud I must be to see the Princess so happy and so much in love.

My last glimpse of Queen Mary that evening was of her regal figure sitting in her car ready to go home. As she crossed the forecourt, she smiled and waved to the waiting crowds. Perhaps, when she sat once more in her own rooms in Marlborough House, she felt, as I did, both sad and happy. A new life for our beloved Princess Elizabeth had begun, as a new life had begun for the beloved Princess May fifty-four years before.

Ten days after Princess May's wedding to Prince George, he wrote from York Cottage to a former naval comrade on the Pacific station: "I can hardly realize yet that I am a married man. . . . All I can say is that I am intensely happy, far happier than I ever thought I could be with anybody. We are spending our honeymoon in this charming little cottage which my father has given me, and it is most comfortable. The peace and rest, after all we went through in London, are heavenly."

They were to spend much more than their honeymoon in the charming little cottage. It was to be their home for many years. All their children, except the Duke of Windsor, were born there.

In London they were given apartments in York House, St. James's Palace, which later were to be occupied by their son as Prince of Wales; but York Cottage was really home to them. As royal residences go, it was small indeed. Formerly used to accommodate the overflow of bachelor guests of the Prince of Wales and Princess Alexandra, it had been known as the Bachelors' Cottage; and some of the bachelors had been known to say that it was "nothing to look at."

Standing well below Sandringham house, and almost hidden in a corner of the deer park, with a lawn and a small lake in front and large trees behind, it is rarely noticed by the Sandringham sightseers. Inside, it is larger than it appears. The large drawing room is almost imposing, but some of the private rooms are small and dark.

The Duke's own sitting-room caught hardly any sun at all; but both he and his bride found the cottage most suitable for the quiet family life they longed to lead.

For us it is important as the place where King George V was born, and where his father, bouncing him on his knee, proudly told the lady-in-waiting, "I have a fine lap."

York Cottage, set among trees and flowering shrubs, had only a tiny garden, but it invited the young Duchess to express the love of flowers that she had shown in her father's garden at Richmond.

From those days until now, in all the homes she has had, Queen Mary has taken a keen interest in the planning, laying out and planting of her gardens. Not long ago, when Dutch tulip growers sent her several hundred bulbs, she accepted them with pleasure, and then spent many happy hours helping to plant them in her garden at Marlborough House.

The present gardens at the King's house at Sandringham are largely of her planning, and whenever she goes there she loves to walk among the flowers and to visit the nearby lavender fields.

One of her great delights at Windsor Castle is the

terraced garden encircling the Round Tower. I have often seen her walking there with Lord and Lady Wigram, who had helped to make the garden so lovely.

London owes a great deal to Queen Mary's love of flowers, for many of the flower beds in the public parks were inspired or suggested by her. The blazing bed of dahlias at Lancaster Gate, Hyde Park, is one of her creations. It is a regular thing, season by season, for her to say "Let us go to Dulwich Park"—or St. James's, or Battersea—"and see how the flower beds are coming on."

That makes, for her, an excursion as interesting as a visit to a museum or an historic building. And of course there is Kew, so near to the scenes of her own childhood, and the more romantic because it was in those beautiful gardens that her father proposed marriage to her mother.

"Queen Mary's Rose Garden" in Regent's Park is one of the sweetest sights of London. There it is easy for anyone to forget that this is almost in the heart of the great city, for it is like a country fairyland, with bank after bank of roses reflected in the still waters of the lake. It was a happy day for Queen Mary when the rose growers of Britain sent her 2,500 new roses for the Regent's Park garden.

Chelsea Flower Show is still one of the greatest events of the year for her, and everyone who sees her there marvels at the endurance she shows in walking for hours among the flowers, enjoying their scent, reading the labels—for her knowledge of the names of flowers and their varieties is almost encyclopædic—and asking questions. I am sure no one could have appreciated more keenly than she did, the kind thought which prompted the organizers of the show to send her an enormous bouquet of roses that had been on exhibition.

And she likes little, humble gardens as well as those which flourish in parks and in large domains. When she visits housing estates, she shows a keen eye for the gardens, and often pays compliments to husbands and wives who have made a brave show of their little space.

Once, when Queen Mary visited me at Nottingham Cottage, Kensington Palace, she gave me good advice about my very small garden. At that time it consisted mostly of some unruly grass and rather depressed looking annuals. "Do dig up the grass," she said, "and have a gay herbaceous border."

I had been in the house only a short time and hadn't been able to make up my mind what to do about the garden. I told Queen Mary that I had thought of planting a hedge. "Well," she said at once, "plant a flowering hedge. Privet is so ugly, and there are so many flowering shrubs." I took her advice, and to-day I have a hedge of lovely forsythia. Queen Mary's advice on gardening is always safe and sound. Among her books at Marlborough House are many volumes on gardening. I remember that morning when she was planning my garden for me, seeing her glance at the walls. Perhaps she was looking for ivy. If she had found any I am sure that she would have called for a pair of shears and snipped it off. If there is anything she dislikes more than privet, it is ivy, which she considers useless and no ornament. No ivy-clad towers for her. Her feud with ivy at Windsor Castle was a war to the death, and she often wielded the knife with her own hand.

For us who know Queen Mary in her later years, it is easy to understand that she settled down happily with her husband in the quiet family life at York Cottage. But sometimes she must have longed to be busier, to take a more useful part in local and national affairs than the custom of the time allowed. Even in her own household affairs!

In all their ways the young Duke and Duchess were overshadowed by the Prince and Princess of Wales, master and mistress of Sandringham House, beside which York Cottage was only "a small house on an estate which drew its inspiration wholly from the Prince and Princess, whereon every smallest happening or alteration was ordered and taken note of by the Prince. The very arrangement of Princess Mary's rooms," we are told, "the planting of her small garden, were matters which required reference to Sandringham House, and the smallest innovation would be regarded with distrust."

Princess Alexandra's beauty, charm and kindliness made her the center of social life, brilliant in its way, but of a sort that could have had no strong appeal to a young woman of Queen Mary's education and upbringing.

Until she married into the Royal Family, no member of it had shown any more than polite interest in artistic and intellectual affairs. For a long time the Royal Family had been self-contained, content to enjoy their high position and to give in return the correct measure of social, ceremonial and political services. Their friends were not philosophers, poets and artists, but people who either had been born to high position or had achieved it in non-intellectual ways. The Duke of York understood them; they were his people and he was quite content with the life of a country gentleman at Sandringham, happy to live so near his mother and sister, whom he loved so much, and to be able to shoot and ride in the Norfolk countryside.

But for the Duchess, full of energy and intellectual curiosity, life at York Cottage must have called for patience, discipline and adjustments to which she had never before been accustomed. If she chafed under this restraint, she showed no sign, but dutifully accepted the part she had been called on to play. What upheld both her and her husband in those first years of testing was their "extraordinary delight in each other."

"May, where are you?" the Duke would cry, running up the stairs after an afternoon in the fields. "Here I am," she would reply. It was a never failing ritual.

At Sandringham for several months each year, one day was like another.

When a baby was coming and the Duchess was in bed, the Duke took up her breakfast at 9 a.m., ate his own at 9.30 and was out of the house by 10 o'clock. The Duke went shooting nearly every day.

After the day's sport he had tea, went through his business papers with the Comptroller and then went to the nursery to say goodnight to the children and hear their prayers. After that he usually played a game of billiards before going to bed.

On Sunday afternoons, he always joined his father for a visit of inspection to the gardens, racing stables and kennels, and to Princess Alexandra's model dairy.

In going round Sandringham and the surrounding villages, the Duchess, with her keen eyes, must have seen many opportunities for useful work in which she would have liked to take a hand, but not only her shyness but also a thousand unwritten rules of procedure restrained her.

Many years later, as Queen Mary, she was to make up for all that, and to set herself heartily to co-operating with the local institutions. Villagers came to know her as a kindly neighbor and friend as well as "the Squire's wife."

There is a story of a servant girl who found herself in distress. No one knows how Queen Mary came to hear of it, but when she did, she behaved as perhaps no Queen before her would have done.

"Poor girl, poor girl!" she said, and without asking any questions, much less hurting the girl more by words of blame, she started at once to see how she could help.

The girl could hardly seek another domestic job without disclosure of her plight. By quiet inquiries, the Queen learned that the girl would like to be a nurse. Then, behind the scenes, the Queen found means to have the girl enter a training course for nurses, and in due course she became a District Nurse, gratefully, for the rest of her life, sharing her secret with the Queen.

There is also a story of a village woman who was ill of a disease so dreadful that neighbours would not go near her for fear of "catching" it. When Queen Mary heard that, she told no one what she intended to do, but that very morning, on returning from a business visit, she called at the cottage and went up to the bedroom with arms full of flowers that she had picked. And she stayed a long time to talk with the sick woman.

Such a thing would have been unheard of in the 'nineties, when the Princess May went to York Cottage as a young bride. But so much was different then. There had been no European War, and even the Boer War was not yet in sight. Queen Victoria was still on the throne, ruling over an Empire whose might had not been challenged. There was no sign of the years of struggle and trial that lay ahead. Life ran in peaceful grooves at

Sandringham as elsewhere, and it seemed certain that it would go on so forever.

At York Cottage, the young Duchess cared for her babies, sewed and knitted by the fireside or in the garden, while her husband read to her books of a sort he had never read before. Books of history and travel; solid and serious books of the Duchess's choice. He began to discover that there were gaps in his own reading, and he made haste to fill them.

It was love in a cottage for these two, who were to bring to Britain and the Empire a conception of royalty that was new in the world. Mary was preparing herself to be the first modern Queen.

PART SIX

OFTEN, in talking with Queen Mary, I have been surprised by some remark of hers showing her knowledge of the everyday problems of British housewives.

They are, of course, different in scale and sometimes in kind from those she has had to meet, living nearly all her life in great houses where housekeeping is a vast enterprise calling for many hands and an intricate organization. That can hardly be called housekeeping in any ordinary sense; and it seems all the more remarkable that she should be so interested in the way we who live in cottages and small houses carry on from day to day.

The mark of her own hands and mind is visible in all the Royal residences—Windsor Castle, Buckingham Palace, Holyrood House, Sandringham House and her present official residence, Marlborough House. As soon as she became Queen, she set out to make the care and arrangement of the royal castles and palaces her own special responsibility.

In Queen Victoria's long reign they had become over-crowded with furniture, pictures and other things, often valuable in themselves, but without proper arrangement. Furniture and hangings were placed without regard to period. Priceless pictures and other treasures were hidden away in cellars and odd corners. All needed a tremendous re-arranging, setting out and cataloguing.

King Edward VII, with the help of expert advisers, began the task, but not much was accomplished in his short reign, and Queen Mary carried on from where he had left off. For her it was not only a labor of love but also what she held to be a patriotic duty, almost a sacred trust.

At Windsor Castle especially, which was the property of the nation, she took over the responsibility of caring for the national treasures. Although she had spent most of her early years in less spacious homes, her travels and reading and the good taste she had inherited from her parents, equipped her well for the great task.

She already knew a good deal about heraldry and antiques, and on that foundation she began to build the knowledge that has made her the recognized authority on pictures, furniture, china, tapestries, silver and objects of art that she is to-day.

Her talent for managing a huge household was soon apparent. She had cupboards, attics and store-rooms turned out, bringing to light many treasures that had been laid away and forgotten. Queen Mary wanted to know the history and meaning of everything, and to have them recorded, so that nothing need ever be mislaid or lost again.

There was, for example, the magnificent dinner set, with Greek and Etruscan figures in sepia on red, with black borders. It had been in one of the china pantries for as long as anyone remembered, but no one could say where it had come from. No record of its acquisition could be found, and the only clue was a vague story that it had been given by an Italian King to a King of England.

Just at that time Queen Mary happened to be reading, in Buckingham Palace, the eighteenth-century novels of Fanny Burney. Some people think Fanny Burney's novels dull, but Queen Mary was finding *Evelina* and *Camilla* extremely useful for the vivid pictures they gave of a period in which she was intensely interested. Suddenly she came to a passage that was far more important to her than the fortunes of Fanny Burney's heroes and heroines. It was only a short paragraph, referring almost casually to a dinner set that had been given to King George III, Queen Mary's great-grandfather.

Was that the dinner set which had puzzled Queen Mary? She decided to find out. Guided by her suggestions, experts searched the records at the British Museum. It was a joyful moment, weeks later, when they were able to place before her the full story of the dinner set.

Made after an ancient model in the Royal potteries of King Ferdinand of the Two Sicilies, it had been presented to King George III in return for his present of two bronze cannon.

With the documents relating to these presents was much information about Greek and Etruscan ware. I am sure that if Queen Mary wished to put her hands on that information at any moment she would know at once where to find it.

Sometimes the search for missing objects led her far from the royal residences.

In the Grand Corridor of Windsor Castle, when Queen Mary first went into residence there, a picture by the celebrated Zoffany showing King George II, Queen Charlotte, and their children had hung for many years. Four of the children, playing with a cockatoo, were apart from the main group.

In the royal collection there was a reproduction, in biscuit china, of that part of the Zoffany picture which showed Queen Charlotte and some of the children. Queen Mary, after considerable search, found another biscuit china piece showing the King as Zoffany had painted him. No one in the castle knew of a third piece to match the others, but Queen Mary felt sure that it had existed, and she hoped that it still could be found.

Art dealers all over the country were asked to search their stocks for a biscuit china reproduction of a picture showing four children and a cockatoo. Before very long the missing piece was found and restored to the royal collection.

Before Queen Mary's time, suites of furniture and sets of pictures, as well as carpets and panelling, had been scattered almost haphazard among the Royal households. At Holyrood and Sandringham she has found chairs that belonged to Windsor, and *vice versâ*. She had them restored to their proper places.

Queen Mary has a thorough knowledge of the contents of every home she has lived in—even Windsor Castle, with its thousand and more rooms, hardly one of which is not filled with objects of beauty and historic interest.

Besides being a beautiful home, Windsor Castle is also a museum of everything that is lovely. The officials there have often spoken to me of how Queen Mary throughout the years sorted out and arranged its contents from chaos into order. The Hon. Sir Richard Molyneux, K.C.V.O., Extra Equerry to Queen Mary and a lifelong and devoted friend, is a connoisseur, and has given her much help in her great, self-imposed task of caring for the nation's treasures.

Both Queen Mary and Sir Richard love every stick and stone of the Castle, and so do I, who have enjoyed the great privilege and honor of living and working there.

For me, there is something almost magical in the fascination of the place. A fortress and home for nearly nine hundred years, it is like a castle in a fairy-tale. The little Princesses loved it too. They knew all about its ghosts, and were not afraid of them.

Windsor's most famous ghost is Herne the Hunter. Both Princess Elizabeth and Princess Margaret have read Harrison Ainsworth's hair-raising story of the apparition of the hanged man, with a stag's antlers on his head, riding through the forest. They were thrilled by the legend, just as they might have been by "Peter Pan."

"What I should like," said Princess Margaret to me, "is to see Herne the Hunter galloping up the East Terrace, some moonlight night, blowing his horn." Everyone in the Castle, including the Princesses, knew the story of the sentry who looked up from his beat and saw the long dead King George III saluting him from an upper window.

There was no attempt to keep such stories from the Princesses; they would have been healthily curious to learn about them for themselves. They were normal children, who loved a good ghost story.

By the way, the tree now called Herne's Oak is not the original one from which Herne the Hunter is supposed to have hanged himself. The old oak, overgrown and gnarled, had been standing since King Henry VIII's time until King George III had it removed and another planted near the site. The second tree was blown down, and Queen Victoria planted another. But Herne the Hunter's ghost, they say, would have nothing to do with substitutes. It was not seen or heard again until King Edward VII planted an oak on the very spot where the first had stood; and since then anyone with very good eyes and ears and a very vivid imagination, given the right sort of night, can see Herne with his antlers and his hounds tearing across the King's private golf course, and can hear the ghostly horn.

Windsor Castle casts a spell over everyone who lives there. King George V, when he first came to the throne, took some time to get over his preference for the simpler, rural delights of Sandringham and Balmoral. Windsor meant grand-scale entertainment and a great deal of formality; the King liked freedom to walk and ride and shoot. Besides, he had an idea that the riverside climate did not suit him.

But Queen Mary's interest in the historic treasures, and her conviction of duty, were infectious, and after a while King George found himself eagerly exploring the castle and reading of its wonders. He never knew as much about the contents of the rooms, galleries, library and archives as Queen Mary, but was always eager to learn. And much of it he learned from her.

Unlike Queen Mary, he hated the idea of changing anything. Without her example, he probably would have left most things as they were. His sitting-room, looking east towards London, was kept just as his father had left it, with red leather chairs, hard sofa, mahogany bookcase and rather commonplace pictures.

When a new housemaid, in his absence, made what she thought were improvements, he summoned the housekeeper, Mrs. Rawlings, and angrily asked her what the girl meant by "putting everything back wrong." Mrs. Rawlings replied: "Well, Your Majesty, be sure it never will be wrong again. I'll get the room photographed." She had almost certainly learned that from Queen Mary, who for many years has made much use of photographs as records.

More than once Sir Richard Molyneux, talking to me of the wonders of Windsor, has said: "I don't believe that any ornament, picture or chair could be moved without Queen Mary's noticing the change at once."

Another loving "guardian" of the Castle is Sir Owen Morshead, K.C.V.O., D.S.O., M.C., Librarian and Assistant Keeper of the King's Archives. He works in the room that was the bedroom of the first Queen Elizabeth, where she held her Levees and received Ambassadors, Archbishops and other dignitaries. During the war, while I was with the Princesses at Windsor Castle, Queen Mary arranged for Sir Owen to take us on tours of the Castle, explaining at each step the historical significance of everything. It was an education for me as much as for the Princesses, who now, if they do not know as much as Queen Mary does about Windsor, are quite as well equipped as she was at the beginning to carry on the gigantic task of royal housekeeping.

Sir Owen has the highest admiration for Queen

Mary's historical knowledge. He showed me once a very old miniature of one of the Kings of England. It was one that had been missing from a set that had been in the castle generations before Queen Mary had found it.

And then, talking of miniatures, there is "Queen Mary's Doll's House," a shining example of her love for little things—sets of tiny furniture, tiny boxes exquisitely wrought and decorated, tiny workboxes hundreds of years old, and a red satin-lined hazel-nut containing a complete sewing set. The Doll's House, which is often on public view, stands on a table in one of the halls of the Castle. It contains beautifully made miniatures of every conceivable thing, all made and presented to Queen Mary by the craftsmen of Britain. Queen Mary has had every one of the contents photographed, and there are two large volumes giving the history of everything, down to the pictures on the walls and the exquisitely woven carpets and rugs.

The Doll's House is a great attraction to visitors from all parts of the world. Queen Mary herself never goes to Windsor without visiting the Doll's House and looking through room after room with never-failing interest. As for the Princesses, when they were small, they thought the Doll's House was the loveliest thing in Windsor Castle.

Windsor on a Sunday afternoon, with the band playing and the people strolling sedately on the paths among the flower beds under the eyes of the King and Queen, is one of the most charming sights on earth. When Princess Elizabeth was a baby, her grandmother would take her in her arms and carry her to a window to see the people, and for them to see her. When the Princesses grew a little older, and played in the Park where they could see and be seen by all, they told me how they enjoyed those Sundays and how they loved the old castle.

On the grounds of the Castle is Frogmore House, filled with memories of King George III and his many daughters, and happier, more recent memories for Queen Mary, who, with King George V, received it as a present from King Edward VII. It was at Frogmore that King George VI and Queen Elizabeth, as Duke and Duchess of York, spent the first few weeks after their wedding, and the young Duchess developed whooping-cough.

Frogmore, with its Royal Mausoleum, is a fascinating place. In the grounds are quaint temples, ginkgo trees and other exotic marvels. To-day the house is a veritable storehouse of Queen Mary's personal possessions.

She loved to drive out there from London, and often, with the Princesses. I have had tea there from the hands of Mrs. Bunning, the housekeeper, who took pride and pleasure in laying a delightful table in the summer house. Mrs. Bunning knew Queen Victoria well, and her fund of information and anecdotes about the old days at Windsor must always have been very interesting to Queen Mary.

I, too, loved to listen, and to go round the house, examining the curious and beautiful objects set out on glass-topped tables. They included mementoes of her many visits to distant lands, including the Delhi Durbar.

In a glass case were Queen Victoria's children's first teeth, mounted like pearls; I wonder how many mothers nowadays preserve such intimate souvenirs? One bracelet always fascinated me. Its links were painted miniatures of the eyes of all Queen Victoria's children.

And loveliest of all to me was to see Queen Mary, erect, dignified, silent, walking under the trees, reliving the days of her youth and the memories of more than sixty years.

But Queen Mary's mind dwells on far more than memories. Preserving the good things that have come to her from the past is important to her, but so is the duty, as she sees it, of keeping to-day's good things for the enjoyment of future generations.

One day, about the time of Princess Elizabeth's wedding, I had been talking with Queen Mary about the many presents the Princess had received throughout her life.

"Wouldn't it be a good idea," said Queen Mary, "to see what Princess Elizabeth has been given in the way of cushions, covers and oddments? I have seen lots of such things on the birthday and Christmas tables, and when one is setting up house all these things can be very useful.

"And the good and nice toys, too. I feel that some of

them should be kept for *future* use. In these days few things that are made in this way equal those that were made in the past, besides being prohibitively expensive.

"I do think also that a few toys which both Princesses have played with ought to be kept as souvenirs. I was always being asked to lend some of my children's toys for exhibitions, just out of interest."

Queen Mary's intense concern for little things as well as great, have given rise to many stories about her so-called domesticity.

There is, for example, the story of the M.P.'s wife, after a visit to Queen Mary at Buckingham Palace, saying, "And I'll guarantee that if we went into her kitchen, it would be just as clean as ours." And I have heard that when Queen Mary first went with her husband to Royal Lodge, Windsor, she looked into all the cupboards and said, "Very clean."

Such legends may have some truth in them, but I do feel that too much stress has been laid on her alleged familiarity with larders, store-cupboards and kitchens. I find it hard to believe, for example, the story of her visiting a Council House, opening a cupboard, inspecting the contents and saying, "Very neat indeed." That would not be like Queen Mary, with her deep respect for other people's homes, and with her endearing shyness.

But I do know what an official of the London Hospital meant when, after she had made an inspection of the hospital of which she is proud to be President, he said: "Queen Mary can never resist an open door." She likes to see everything that is going on, when what is going on is something that she has made her special concern; and an open door is an invitation.

At Windsor Castle there is a vast kitchen garden, the produce from which must be sufficient to supply the vegetable needs of all the royal houses. Mrs. Bruce, who holds the important position of Housekeeper at the Castle, has a room lined with cupboards filled with perfectly bottled fruits and endless jars of jams and jellies.

I am sure that Queen Mary has always enjoyed her visits to that room. It is something after her own heart. It is not only arranged with meticulous precision, but has also a lovely color scheme. There are bottles of deep yellow peaches contrasting beautifully with rows of blood-red plums, all as good to look at as to eat. I have often thought that Mrs. Bruce's store cupboards would make a splendid subject for an artist.

I well remember Queen Mary's first visit to me in my own little home, Nottingham Cottage, almost next door to her own birthplace, Kensington Palace. It was soon after my marriage. She sent me a note asking if I would be at home on the following afternoon, as she would like to call and see me.

When her chauffeur rang the door-bell, I saw that he had a parcel in his hand; he laid it on the hall table. "A little gift for you, my dear," said Queen Mary. How thoughtful it was of Her Majesty to remember that in my native Scotland, as in parts of Northern England, it is the friendly custom, on visiting a house for the first time, to "handsel" the house—that is, to bring a present. In this case the gift was a Dundee cake which had come from Canada.

But of course Queen Mary was not visiting Nottingham Cottage for the first time. She had known it from her childhood. She went with me through all the familiar rooms, recalling to her mind every cupboard and corner. "You ought to have some pictures for your walls," she said. "Do come over to Marlborough House and choose some."

A little later I did so. For a little while I hesitated between some flower pictures in water color and a set of the twelve famous "Cries of London" prints, and at last I voted for flowers. Next day the pictures were delivered to my home. With them came two men to hang them—another example of Queen Mary's extreme thoughtfulness. And she herself called to see how the pictures looked on my walls.

One day Sir Charles Kenderdine, creator of the Roehampton Hospital for limbless soldiers, found Queen Mary with her sleeves rolled up, happily and energetically hanging pictures in Buckingham Palace.

Those who have seen Queen Mary, at Holyrood, helping in the re-arrangement of furniture and carpets have been surprised at the capacity she showed for such tasks.

But I see in all this not mere domesticity, a love of house-work in itself, but part and parcel of the efficiency and thoroughness with which she has tackled every task. It is part of "the grand manner" which is so natural to her —in fact, second nature.

So also is her understanding of the problems that all British housewives have had to meet.

I am reminded now of a characteristically thoughtful remark she made to two hospital Sisters, who, having cared for her at one time, were invited to Marlborough House, given presents and then shown round the place. Queen Mary pointed out that the stuffing was coming out of some chairs. "How difficult it is," she said, "in these days to keep one's house in order and get repairs done." That was at a time when it was difficult to buy anything for a house; one had to have the necessary units.

My own marriage took place during that time, and one day when I was having tea with Queen Mary at Marlborough House, I spoke to her of my furnishing problems. She was well aware of the difficulties that all of us were facing, with shortages of soap, house-linen and other things. She said to me: "You must have the name and address of a man I discovered, who mends and re-covers chairs very beautifully." She went to her desk and wrote down the particulars. The man was a crafts-man working in a small way on his own, having been disabled in the First World War.

Queen Mary goes to a great deal of trouble to choose

a present for anyone. She likes to be sure of giving something that the recipient really likes and perhaps has wanted for some time. On one occasion, as a Christmas present, I received from Queen Mary the most happy surprise that I could imagine. When I opened the box and unpacked a lovely blue bedside lamp, I remembered that Queen Mary, in visiting my house, had noticed that in one bedroom there was no lamp beside the bed. Not only had she noticed that, but also the blue walls and decorations. And the blue of the lamp was a perfect match.

Much of the tidiness, punctuality, thrift and industry which would have made Queen Mary a great success in any sphere of life must have been in her character in the days when, as Duchess of York, she was a young house-wife at York Cottage, Sandringham. And this time I mean *everything* that the word housewife implies.

She was perhaps the first Queen in history to interest herself deeply in the details of running her own house, and that, perhaps, was because the house was small enough to invite such interest and to give her the opportunity to indulge it. And certainly it also sprang from that conviction of duty which has always upheld and guided her.

There was not even a spare room at York Cottage. When there were guests, accommodation had to be found for them in other parts of the estate. Nearly all the servants had to be boarded out.

When the Duke of York was asked where the servants

slept, he said that he himself had often wondered about that very thing, and had come to the conclusion that they roosted in the trees.

Before the Duke and Duchess went there, York Cottage had no billiard room. But while the house was being got ready, the Duchess had seen that a billiard table was installed, because she knew that her husband enjoyed the restful pastime which was the favorite recreation of Herbert Spencer and other philosophers.

"Pushing those little balls about" could not have had much appeal to the young Duchess, but she set out to master the game, and before long she could often beat her husband at it.

When Queen Mary's mother, the Duchess of Teck, visited York Cottage for the first time she found it delightful, and wrote to a friend: "This is the perfection of an ideal cottage. Each room is charming in its way, and everything in perfect taste and most cosy and comfortable."

The daughter's enthusiasm was more restrained. "The Cottage," she wrote, "is very nice, but so small for present uses." She was to feel its smallness even more when it had to hold six growing children. But in the first years of marriage she went happily about the business of running the house.

This she did in a most businesslike way, seeing that all household bills were paid at once, that there was always plenty of fresh air in the rooms and that linen and hangings were kept in perfect repair.

I have been told that she knew all the contents of her linen cupboards, counted every item and personally kept lists, and that she gave the same attention to the contents of the Royal larder.

Everything ran like clockwork at York Cottage. Meals were served exactly on time. Every day the young Duchess inspected the kitchen and planned the simple meals that both she and the Duke of York preferred to the elaborate fare of the other Royal houses.

This was in the 'nineties, an age of plenty. All that neatness and punctuality was quite to the taste of her sailor husband, accustomed to having everything ship-shape. "May is so understanding," said the Duke often to his friends.

But, of course, the life of the Duke and Duchess at York Cottage was often interrupted by public duties, which soon came thick and fast. In the first summer following their wedding, some of the Royal Family made many visits of inspection to the Cottage after small dinner parties. Later the Duke and Duchess went to Cowes, where Kaiser Wilhelm was enjoying the racing from his yacht, *Hohenzollern*. The Duke raced his yacht, the famous *Britannia*, with which his career as a yachtsman was always to be linked.

In September, the Royal couple went to Edinburgh to receive the wedding gift subscribed for by the citizens and to open the new wing of the Hospital for Incurables.

Then they were the guests of Lord and Lady Londonderry at Stockton-on-Tees. There they opened a park, before going on to York to make acquaintance with the ancient city from which they took their title.

Wherever they went, they were joyously received. The Duchess, although public appearances were still ordeals for her, accompanied her husband whenever she could—even when she could have found excuses to stay at home and lead the quiet life that she loved.

In October there came a lull in the rush of public duties, and the Duke and Duchess returned to the cottage to settle down for the winter.

On the last day of the year, an invitation was received from the Governor of Victoria, New South Wales, for the Duke and Duchess to visit Australia. This invitation had to be declined for a reason which could not be announced at the time.

In the following June, the Duchess of York arrived at White Lodge for a prolonged stay with her mother, the Duchess of Teck. Three weeks later the Duke of York wrote in his diary:

"White Lodge, 23rd June.—At 10 o'clock a sweet little boy was born and weighed 8 lbs. Mr. Asquith came to see him."

Mr. Asquith was then Home Secretary. The dear little boy was the future Duke of Windsor.

PART SEVEN

"The Queen and I." We all are accustomed now to that Royal way of speaking. It seems to us natural that King George VI, in talking to us on the radio, should refer thus to Queen Elizabeth, and so remind us that she shares his sentiments and aspirations and is always by his side.

But it was not always so with our Kings and Queens.

Before Queen Mary's time the part played by a Queen Consort in a King's public affairs—if indeed she played any part—was given little recognition in formal address.

In those days, for a King to have spoken of "The Queen and me" in a public speech would have been a startling departure from custom.

King George V, from the beginning of his reign to the end, spoke of Queen Mary in that way, so linking her with his life and public work. In his first broadcast, from the British Empire Exhibition at Wembley on St. George's Day, 1924, he paid her that tribute of courtesy.

It seemed so natural to the man, and so in keeping with what everyone knew about the exemplary Royal couple, that no one remarked on the innovation except to exclaim, "Wasn't that a nice thing to say!" And King George went on saying it at every opportunity for the rest of his life.

It may seem a little matter, but surely it is highly significant of the extraordinary changes in public life that have come to pass since the days when the young Duchess of York, the future Queen Mary, was bringing up her children at York Cottage, in the shadow of the great country house at Sandringham which was becoming the center of a glittering social circle.

Of all her six children, only Edward, the first child, was not born in Norfolk. His christening, in the drawing room of the Duchess of Teck's house, White Lodge, Richmond Park, was an historic occasion for the number of illustrious personages who were brought together there.

Queen Victoria invited all her Royal relatives who could come, including the future Czar and Czarina.

The sponsors were Queen Victoria, the Prince and Princess of Wales, the Cesarewitch, the Duke of Cambridge, the Duke and Duchess of Teck, the Duchess of Fife (representing the Queen of Denmark), Princess Victoria of Wales (representing the Queen of the Hellenes), Princess Adolphus of Teck (representing the King of Denmark), the Duke of Connaught (representing the Duke of Würtemberg) and Prince Louis of Battenberg (representing the Duke of Saxe-Coburg and Gotha).

The baptism was performed by the Archbishop of Canterbury, assisted by two other clergymen.

The christening font, a gold bowl of exquisite design, mounted on a pedestal covered with scarlet cloth, stood in a window overlooking Richmond Park.

The baby Prince, wearing the Honiton lace robe made for the Queen's eldest daughter, was carried into the room by his nurse and handed first to the lady-in-waiting. Then Queen Victoria placed the baby in the hands of the Archbishop, who named him Edward Albert Christian George Andrew Patrick David.

Even more significant than this array of noble names was the great mass of letters and telegrams that came to the Duke and Duchess from the ends of the earth to testify to the affection that they had inspired in all sorts of people.

In the Duke's replies and in other writings of those early years of marriage he showed how happy he was to be able to spend most of his time with his family in their country home.

But of course they had duties that often took them away. In the early autumn they made State visits to Birmingham, to lay the foundation stone of the General

Hospital, to Liverpool, to open the new Post Office and to Leeds, to open the School of Medicine and inaugurate the new central hall and library.

And in November, the Duke again had to tear himself from Sandringham to attend the old Czar's funeral and the young Czar's wedding, and then to pay an official visit to Berlin.

The very mention of these foreign visits is a reminder of the gulf between the world of the 'nineties and the world of to-day—a gulf that is bridged by Queen Mary's long and steadfast life.

But even then the Duke and Duchess, as far as their position permitted, had begun to set a new pattern for Royalty. In Petersburg in particular, the Duke alarmed the court officials and police by his insistence on seeing places that were not on the official program.

That winter at Sandringham brought the great frost of 1895, which old people still remember and talk about.

It must have been great fun for Princess Alexandra, who, with her Scandinavian upbringing, was an accomplished skater.

There were skating parties on the ice there and on the lake at Buckingham Palace, and the young Duchess of York was soon able to hold her own skates. But the end of March found her at the task of helping to nurse her husband through a sharp attack of influenza, from which he recovered slowly.

That was a duty which was often to fall to the Duchess. Years later, a letter addressed simply "Mrs. Queen" came to her at Buckingham Palace. It was from a woman who said how very sorry she was that "your husband has got bronchitis," and conveyed this practical advice:

"Rub your husband's chest with camphorated oil when the bronchial signs appear. I always do. It is a remedy I have never known to fail."

"How good of her to think of me, and realize my anxiety," said Queen Mary.

The summer following the birth of Prince Edward brought for the Duke and Duchess another round of ceremonial duties.

In June, after seeing Lord Rosebery, then Prime Minister, win the Derby, the Duke raced his yacht *Britannia* to victory in the Cinque Ports Regatta, and then went to Germany as the guest of the Kaiser for the opening of the Kiel Canal.

Our present King George VI was born in the small white bedroom at York Cottage on December 14th.

The entry in his father's diary reads: "A little boy was born weighing nearly 8 lbs. at 3.40 (S.T.). Everything most satisfactory, both doing very well. Sent a great number of telegrams, had something to eat. Went to bed at 6.45 very tired."

"S.T." means Sandringham Time. The Prince of Wales, long before the invention of Daylight Saving, followed the country custom of keeping all clocks advanced half an hour.

December 14th was the anniversary of the death of the Prince Consort, and had for many years been a day of mourning for Queen Victoria. But this time her grief was turned to gladness.

"This terrible anniversary returned for the 34th time," she wrote. "Found telegrams from Georgie and Sir J. Williams, saying that dear May had been safely delivered of a son at three this morning. Georgie's first feeling was regret that this dear child should be born on such a sad day. I have a feeling that it may be a blessing for the dear little boy, and may be looked upon as a gift from God."

So, surely, it has proved to be. I cannot help thinking now that the birth of Prince George on that day of days was a happy event that was needed to bring Queen Victoria completely back to public life and to persuade her to make her Diamond Jubilee in 1897 the great popular festival that it was.

Prince George's christening, at the Sandringham Parish Church, was a much less elaborate affair than that of Prince Edward had been. The Bishop of Norwich performed the ceremony.

The third child, Princess Mary, the present Princess Royal, was born on April 25th, 1897—in the year of the great Jubilee. The gold cup used at the christening, in Sandringham Parish Church, was the wedding gift of the City of Edinburgh.

Three more children were to be born to the Duchess

of York at Sandringham. No wonder she and the Duke always loved the place!

On June 22nd, 1897, Queen Victoria had reigned sixty years—far longer than any other British monarch in history. The Diamond Jubilee, with an imposing procession through the streets of London to St. Paul's Cathedral, and bonfires, fireworks and other celebrations all over the country, was the culminating event of a brilliant season. The Duchess of York was seen at all the Court functions in honor of the event, and in the procession she made her first public appearance in any State pageant since her marriage.

At the Golden Jubilee, ten years before, she had had only an inconspicuous place in the procession; even so the crowds had acclaimed her as the popular "Princess May."

But this time she rode in the carriage only a few paces behind the Queen's State coach. Dressed in the summery pastel colors that have always become her so well, in mature years as in youth, she was welcomed as heartily as she had been when a bride.

It has been so all her life. In all the Royal processions in which she has appeared in our time, even when she has not been the principal figure, there has been a special welcome for her from the crowds.

I have seen it on such occasions as the Silver Wedding celebrations of our present King and Queen, and the Wedding of Princess Elizabeth—that sudden happy smile of Queen Mary's that expresses her surprise that so many people should be pleased to see her.

On that day of the Diamond Jubilee she had yet another reason to be happy. Her mother, the Duchess of Teck, making her first public appearance after recovering from a serious operation, was accorded a great reception by the crowd.

For the Duchess of York was still very close to her mother, with whom she and the children went often to stay at the White Lodge, Richmond Park, the Duchess's own childhood home.

At a grand Jubilee Ball given by the Duchess of Devonshire at Devonshire House, the Prince of Wales got himself up in all the bravery of the Grand Prior of the Order of Jerusalem, and his lovely Princess Alexandra was more beautiful than ever in the role of Margot de Valois, Queen of Navarre.

The Duchess of York was content to appear as a lady of Margot's court and the Duke as Clifford, Earl of Cumberland. The Duke was not very fond of such affairs; no doubt he would have been happier shooting at Sandringham.

Sir Henry Irving, the famous actor, in the red robes of Cardinal Wolsey, was heard to remark: "These ladies and gentlemen look very fine, but they have not quite got inside their characters."

It was in the eighteen-nineties, in the early years of her married life, that Queen Mary began to show the interest in the theater and its people which has stayed with her all her life.

Thanks to her mother's appreciation of good acting, Princess May, even as a girl, was personally acquainted with the greatest players of the day.

After a performance of "Charles the First," by W. G. Wills, she was offered by Sir Henry Irving a lock of King Charles's hair.

Sir Charles Wyndham and his wife had the honor more than once of entertaining the Princess and her mother at supper after the theater. Beerbohm Tree was another actor whose work and society they enjoyed.

In those days, thanks to Queen Victoria's use of the Court Circular to make known all the activities of the Royal Family, every visit to the theatre was a semi-official affair, duly recorded thus: "Their Royal Highnesses the . . . visited . . . Theater last night and honored the performance of . . . with their presence."

There is no such formality nowadays. When the King and Queen decide to go to a theater or the movies they have their seats ordered by telephone in the ordinary way, and people in the stalls, without any previous warning, may find them moving to their seats beside them.

And if the stalls are full, the King and Queen are content to have places found for them in some other part of the house. In this they follow the precedent set by Queen Mary, who, with all her insistence on the observance of proper ceremony, as a matter of duty, dislikes unnecessary fuss.

In some ways the so-called Gay Nineties were straitlaced.

When Victorian young ladies went bathing they wore more clothes than the average girl of to-day wears in summer in the street. When they went to the theater their elders had to be assured that they would see and hear nothing stronger than harmless farce, drawing-room comedy, or "wholesome" melodrama.

Just before Princess May's wedding, the Duchess went to see Pinero's "The Second Mrs. Tanqueray," which was then considered a "daring" play because the heroine was a woman who was not exactly married.

"My daughter will be able to see this play next month," said the Duchess of Teck.

A little later she did; and many years after then, when "The Second Mrs. Tanqueray" was revived by Gladys Cooper, Queen Mary persuaded her husband to see it too.

Her patronage of a "problem" play in the 'nineties, when the only imaginable problem was a triangle, had much the same effect as her going unexpectedly to see the more recent play, "Pick-Up Girl," which presented a much more startling problem in a far more outspoken way.

But surely this evidence of Queen Mary's broadmindedness could have surprised no one who knew of her intense interest in all matters concerning the welfare of young people.

She had heard that "Pick-Up Girl" was concerned with juvenile delinquents and their sex troubles, and no doubt she had been told also that it contained frank language and actions that some people might consider unfit for her to witness.

But prudishness is as foreign to Queen Mary's nature as any other sort of snobbery. If she was shocked by the play, she did not say so, but allowed it to be known that she had seen it. And then the play was moved from a small theater in Notting Hill to become a West End success.

The 'nineties and the early 1900's were a golden age of musical comedy, the heyday of the Gaiety Theatre and Daly's, when everyone was whistling and humming tunes from "The Geisha," "San Toy," "The Country Girl" and "The Belle of New York."

Such music must ring happily in Queen Mary's memory, for it recalls the years when she and her husband, not yet King and Queen, were free enough from affairs of State to go often to the theater together.

In later years there was to be less time for such entertainment, but since the end of the Second World War Queen Mary has resumed her theater visits, and has shown increasing interest in the movies.

Often she has sat in a back row of a movie theater, unknown to the rest of the audience. That was how she saw, for example, "Monsieur Vincent," the film of the life of St. Vincent de Paul, at the Curzon.

When, as happens to so many of us, she finds she has missed the "first run" of a good film, she will go to a suburban theater to catch it; that was how she saw "Anna and the King of Siam" and later the Arnhem film, at the Gaumont State at Kilburn. And she went to Kilburn again to a Children's Cinema Club show on a Saturday morning.

Broadminded Queen Mary was greatly amused when, having seen the première of "The Wicked Lady," she learned that, to spare her ears, a certain naughty word had been cut out of the sound-track.

She liked the show so much that she went to see it again. What interested her in the picture in the first place was that the scene of the action, where much of the film was shot, was Blickling Hall, the Norfolk home of the late Marquis of Lothian, and well known to Queen Mary. It is known to history too, for in the grounds of Blickling Hall, Henry VIII courted Anne Boleyn.

During the war, when Queen Mary was at Badminton in Gloucestershire, many films were shown in the great hall to audiences of troops and villagers. Everyone, including Queen Mary, paid threepence for admission; for a full-length showing of "Gone with the Wind" that was surely a bargain price. Often the company had a song-fest thrown in, Queen Mary joining happily in "Swanee River," "John Brown's Body" and other community songs.

There is no private projection room in Marlborough House, because there is no room that is really suitable for it. But once, before the war, Queen Mary had the dining room wired for sound for a performance of "Good-bye Mr. Chips" before a small audience that included the domestic staff.

Queen Mary's interest in movies took her once to the Denham Studios, where she saw how everything was done, watched a scene "shot" and amused some of the players by confessing that, although she enjoyed the movies, she could never remember the names of the stars.

That must be the one blank spot in that extraordinary memory of hers, the workings of which have so often astonished me. It goes back so far, and is so crowded with names, faces and incidents, that to talk with her is always to learn more about the world as it was and is.

And how different is the modern world of movies, television, atomic warfare and the threat of universal upheaval from the calm, settled era of hope and progress into which Queen Mary's children were born!

No writer, no speaker, no prophet of those days gave any sign of understanding that a golden age was ending. It may have been golden only for a few, but "for every class in the State there was the compensation of hope and evidence of improvement to come.

"The workers saw a new light of dawn, the privileged a summer sun still high in the heavens." And wages were paid in golden sovereigns, each worth twenty silver shillings. The British Empire, the greatest the world had ever seen, had no rival in sight. Bands played "Rule Britannia" and "Soldiers of the Queen":

> *And when we say we've always won,*
> *And when they ask us how it's done,*
> *We proudly point to every one*
> *Of England's soldiers of the Queen!*

There was plenty of Imperial bounce in the British people, and plenty of justification for it. Many years of peace had given them a settled feeling of permanence and security.

Nobody could have guessed that the Duke and Duchess of York, bringing up their family in the cottage at Sandringham, were destined to face the trials and tribulations that a world war would bring to their country.

Still less could anyone have seen that they were to set a new pattern for Royalty, and to take the lead in molding a new conception of Empire.

Perhaps it was because home and family meant so much to them, that they were among the first to see the British people as a family and the British Commonwealth as a family of peoples.

In the August following the Diamond Jubilee, the Duke and Duchess paid a visit to Ireland, and their activities there were a foreshadowing of the new spirit.

In a dress of green poplin and a toque of cream lace,

green poppies and pink roses, the Duchess was enthusiastically acclaimed as she and the Duke drove through the streets of Dublin. Then, instead of giving all their time to ceremonial and social business, they spent hours at the Textile Exhibition, which they opened. The Duchess was so pleased with what she saw that she insisted on going again.

Even the Dublin Horse Show had less appeal for her than the Textile Exhibition. She walked through gallery after gallery, inspecting embroidery and needlework, and showed the greatest interest in the beautiful work done by poor children in convents and industrial homes. She bought several pieces, and particularly admired the sheets and bedspreads in drawn threadwork and also the hem-stitching done by Irish country folk in their cabins.

The Viceroy (the Earl of Cadogan) said that he could hardly drag the Duchess away. That, surely, was a glimpse of the indefatigable Queen Mary we know today.

From Dublin, the Duke and Duchess went to Killarney and other beauty spots, but I am sure that the Duchess got more satisfaction out of the visit to the great shipyards and linen factories of Belfast, where she surprised officials by asking all sorts of technical questions and by wanting to see much more than was on the scheduled program. Especially she wanted to see how the work was done.

And then a great sorrow came to Queen Mary.

Immediately after her return from Ireland she went to White Lodge to see her mother, the beloved Duchess of Teck, whom she found greatly changed. Mother and daughter went to church together at Kingston Vale, and on the way back the older woman complained of feeling cold and ill.

She was better in the afternoon, but when the doctor came the next morning he strongly urged her not to carry out her intention of going to a London theater that night.

"But I must go," she said. "The manager has taken so much trouble to get back the box for us, and I cannot bear to disappoint him."

Later she had changed her mind, and she sent the Duke of Teck and Prince Alexander, his son, to represent her. The Duchess of York remained to keep her mother company and to entertain her with stories of her visit to Ireland, with rapturous descriptions of the lovely lace and embroidery, the hospitality of the people and the magnificent scenery.

Next day the Duchess of Teck tried to get up but had to go back to bed. In the afternoon an operation was performed. She seemed to recover but soon was seen to be failing.

During the night she lost consciousness, but for a moment she opened her eyes, saw her daughter by the bedside and smiled. Then she went to sleep and died.

And here is what an old servant said about the Duchess of Teck and her daughter: "When a tea was given to the people after Prince Edward was born, the Duchess of Teck came down to the field, and, seeing me, said, 'Oh, here's mother Ann,' and came up and shook hands with me, and made so much of me that all around were quite jealous.

"Ah! She was good. And she didn't forget me at Princess May's wedding, but sent me some wedding cake. Prince Alexander himself brought it to me at my cottage in the lane.

"Once when I was out in the stable-yard, cleaning, Princess May opened the schoolroom window and threw me out a scarlet petticoat, saying 'That's for you, mother Ann. I made it for you.' And it was a beauty.

"No; there wasn't any pride in any of them.

"And to think that now the Duchess is gone! I went up to the Lodge afterwards, and the Duke and Duchess of York came out and spoke to me; the Duke of Teck was in the corridor; he just touched my shoulder, but he could not speak."

More sorrow was in store for Queen Mary. The shock of her mother's death completely unnerved her father, who was not seen in public again after the funeral.

For the short remainder of his life he remained in strictest seclusion at White Lodge, where his daughter often went to care for him. She was hastening to his bedside when the news came that he was dying, and she arrived too late to see him again alive.

The Boer War had begun. The Duchess of York's three brothers were fighting in South Africa.

In a few weeks she was to become the mother of a fourth child. During her father's illness, little had been done about the administration of her mother's affairs. Now she had to shoulder not only that burden but also that of winding up her father's estate.

In those tasks the Duchess showed not only her mastery of details, but also consummate tact and a capacity for business affairs that surprised those who had not expected to see such qualities in one who had been brought up as a Princess.

We who know Queen Mary now are well aware of her keen eye for detail, her tidiness of habit and mind, and her thoroughgoing way of tackling any task that is before her. But it must have been a revelation to those who saw her at work fifty years ago.

"Many points of difficulty arose from time to time in connection with the administration of the two estates," wrote one who was associated with her in the business. "In due course these were laid before the Duchess of York, who quickly grasped their meaning, and arrived at decisions at once rapid and sound.

"This rendered comparatively easy the work of those entrusted with the details, and they had the encouragement of knowing that Her Royal Highness was never slow to express appreciation of the efforts made to fulfil her commands."

And then she returned to York Cottage, where, on March 3rd, 1900, Prince Henry was born. "I am delighted with my small son," the Duchess wrote, "but so anxious about my brothers, who are still in South Africa."

Lord Roberts came home from South Africa to be the baby's godfather. For each of her six children, five of whom were born in the small white bedroom at York Cottage, the Duchess kept a notebook where she recorded weights, first teeth and first words, and preserved locks of hair.

Until that time, the public appearances of Royal children were occasions almost as ceremonious as those of their elders. They were never allowed for a moment to forget that they were Princes and Princesses. Even their daily airings in the park were duly recorded in the Court Circular.

It was not so with Queen Mary's children. They were brought up to live quietly, with family prayers, church attendance, regular lessons, pocket money that they had to account for, walks in the country, and, above all, the society and guidance of their parents.

King George took them on his knee and taught them jingles, such as William Allingham's:

> *Up the airy mountain,*
> *Down the rushy glen,*
> *We daren't go a-hunting*

For fear of little men.
Wee folk, good folk,
Trooping all together;
Green jacket, red cap,
And white owl's feather.

They stole little Bridget
For seven years long;
When she came down again
Her friends were all gone.
They took her lightly back
Between the night and the morrow,
They thought she was fast asleep,
But she was dead with sorrow.

In those days the complaint was often heard—but not from the Duke or Duchess—that York Cottage was not a suitable country house for the heir to the throne. But the Duke in particular was devoted to the place.

When Sir Arthur Ponsonby, his Secretary, pointed out that the cottage was unsuitable for entertaining on the scale which the Duke's position demanded, he replied that that was just as well. He and the Duchess were happy there, with their growing family.

But the time was coming soon when all this would have to change. The South African war was dragging on longer than anyone had expected, and the strain was telling on Queen Victoria, then aged eighty-one.

The deaths of a son and a grandson increased her burden. For a few weeks her health seemed to improve, and the Duke of York wrote: "Thank God the Queen is better now, but she has been quite seedy." But her eyesight was failing, and so, it seemed, were her spirits.

When Lord Roberts sent the Household Cavalry home from South Africa, Queen Victoria inspected the First Life Guards on their arrival at Windsor. In the carriage with her was the Duchess of York, to greet her brother, the new Duke of Teck, who was an officer in the regiment.

That proved to be the last military ceremony in which Queen Victoria would take part. Soon she went to her country house at Osborne, Isle of Wight, and there she died.

"I saw her peaceful end," wrote the Duchess of York.

The Duke of York wrote:

"At 2.30 we were all again sent for and remained with darling Grandmamma almost the whole time until 6.30, when our beloved Queen and Grandmamma, one of the greatest women that ever lived, passed peacefully away, surrounded by her sorrowing children and grandchildren.

"She was conscious up to 5 o'clock and called each of us by name and we took leave of her and kissed her hand; it was terribly distressing. Thank God darling May arrived in time, at 5.30, to see her.

"I shall never forget that scent in her room with all

of us sobbing and heartbroken round her bed. We all went to her room at 10 o'clock and there she lay, covered with flowers, looking so beautiful and peaceful.

"The Bishop of Winchester read some prayers and we all knelt round the bed."

Between the Queen and the Duchess there had always been a strong tie. As a child "Princess May" had a high place in the Queen's heart, and was always welcome at Windsor.

As she grew up, she became more and more attached to the Queen, who inspired in her affection as well as the awe and admiration one so exalted was bound to command from a junior Princess.

In a letter to a friend after the funeral, mentioning the flowers the royal children had sent, the Duchess of York wrote: "I talked to them about the dear Queen, so that they may never forget their grandmother."

Some observers have noted many points of resemblance between Queen Mary and Queen Victoria.

Sir George Arthur, for example, detects "the same conduct of life based on broad and sound principles, the same high courage and resolute willpower, the same inflexible uprightness mated to the most courteous manners, the same dislike of anything sensational or *outré*, the same prodigious memory, with everything docketed and available for reference at a moment's notice . . . the same common sense so developed as to reach almost to the edge of genius . . . the same sincere, reverent religion, the same belief that children should be tended with affection and brought up in the fear of God."

But, Sir George Arthur pointed out, "Queen Victoria, rightly careful of her own comfort, was, quite unconsciously, little concerned with the comfort of others except of her own personal dependents.

"Ministers were compelled with great inconvenience to make long journeys and cross boisterous waters in windy weather rather than the Sovereign should put herself out to be at Windsor in time of political crisis; she regretted that she could not ask Mr. Gladstone to 'sit down,' although the old statesman had every need to be spared fatigue. . . .

"So in minor matters; no attempt was made to render Queen Victoria's afternoon drawing-rooms anything else than truly formidable affairs, especially for *décolletées* dowagers who perhaps in streaming sunlight had been exposed for a couple of hours to ribald remarks from a crowd.

"No refreshments were offered, not from any motive of economy, but because it was thought that they would give to a Court ceremonial the flavour of an entertainment.

"Nor was the Queen concerned with the disappointment of the majority of the ladies, and especially the debutantes, who never saw her at all, as she usually left the Throne Room long before the defile of dipping dames and damsels had passed. . . .

"But what is far more important, Queen Victoria knew nothing of any class below the middle class and of these not very much. . . .

"She was deeply concerned with the welfare of her people at large, but she never seems to have formed any mental picture of the millions of mournful workers with neither sufficient light nor food, and even the semi-starvation which prevailed immediately before the repeal of the Corn Laws, provoked, so far as one reads her published correspondence, no passionate expressions of pity."

How different is Queen Mary from that picture!

Everyone who knows her has experience of her self-effacing consideration for the comfort of others. She would rather put herself to inconvenience than let a guest or a friend suffer it.

At her Courts, she went to great trouble to see that as many as possible were personally recognized by her. It was she who made the arrangements for the ladies to find shelter in the Palace, away from the crowd.

Most striking of all is the contrast between Queen Victoria's apparent blindness to social conditions and Queen Mary's intense interest in the living and working conditions of the people.

To our grandfathers, the death of Queen Victoria must have seemed almost like the end of the world. The sharpness of the break was the more abrupt because it did mark the end of a wonderful century.

How magically Noel Coward captured the solemn spirit of the hushed crowd on the day of Queen Victoria's funeral in that scene in "Cavalcade." For those who had lived in that age a curtain had fallen.

But for the new generation, the curtain was rising on a new century, with new ways of living and thinking.

For Queen Mary herself a new life was about to begin. A few weeks after the death of Queen Victoria she and her husband were to leave their home and their children and travel to the ends of the earth.

PART EIGHT

It was hard for me to realize, at my first meeting with King George V and Queen Mary, on the lawn of the Royal Lodge, Windsor Great Park, that the King had only recently recovered from a long, dangerous and exceedingly painful illness. True, he carried a walking stick, but did not use it for support, and certainly he did not look like a man who had been at death's door only a few months before.

I don't think it entered my head at the time, perhaps because I was so overwhelmed by the occasion and by Their Majesties' evident desire to put me at ease; but later, when I was alone, the full force of it struck me.

This was the King for whom the whole Empire had been praying, who had fought death for months, for whom a thanksgiving service had been held in Westminister Abbey and who had received a wonderful manifestation of the people's love and loyalty.

And I remembered that while I had been reading and hearing of all this, back home in Scotland, sharing the general anxiety and relief, (but never dreaming that I should ever set eyes on the King and Queen, much less talk with them) my thoughts turned to Queen Mary, who had been by her husband's side through the long ordeal.

What had it all meant to her? We know what other Queens have thought and felt. Queen Victoria, who lost her husband when she was young, poured her heart into her *Journals* which we all can read.

As we know, Queen Mary also keeps a diary, in which she writes every day, but no one but herself knows what she writes in it. Perhaps posterity may learn, but while she lives, she asks no one to share any of the many sorrows she has suffered.

I know of no complaining word that has ever passed her lips; her only references to sad events in her own life have been gracious acknowledgments of public expressions of sympathy. I have told you how happy she always seems; I have never seen her otherwise, even at times when her heart must have been heavy with grief.

Soon after King George's recovery from that illness, writes Mr. John Gore, his officially authorized biographer, "someone . . . asked Sir Farquhar Buzzard (the

famous physician) who of those round the King in his
crisis had 'really saved his life.'

"Sir Farquhar replied instantly, 'The Queen.'

"He went on to explain that the Queen's complete
faith in and loyalty to the doctors in attendance ensured
that they could do their work without fuss, without
interference and without being compelled to consider
a mass of well-intentioned advice from outside."

Queen Mary would have made a first-class nurse. She
has all the natural qualities, and much of the skill and
knowledge also.

In her time she has had a great deal to do with sick-
ness. Considering that she herself has hardly ever been
ill in her life, her patience and sympathy with invalids
is extraordinary.

She showed these qualities even as a child. When any
poor person in the neighborhood of her mother's home,
The White Lodge, Richmond Park, fell ill and needed
help, Princess May would hurry to the sufferer's bedside.

As Duchess of York, as Princess of Wales, as Queen
and as Queen Mother, she had been a Lady Bountiful,
not to a neighborhood only, but to hospitals and institutions of many sorts and especially those which are
concerned with the welfare of women and children.

"Many a poor mother," wrote Sir Clement Kinloch-
Cooke forty years ago, "has been helped in the time of
her trouble out of Queen Mary's bounty, and many a
young man and woman owe their present position in life

to a kindness received from Queen Mary in the days of their childhood."

Since then, visiting hospitals in two great wars, and in the years between, she has witnessed far more pain and suffering than most of us. And it has never been easy for Queen Mary.

Schooled to avoid any show of her own feelings, she is extremely sensitive inwardly, and I know that it is a great effort for her to go among the sick and hurt. Yet she never flinches.

The great London Hospital, in the heart of the East End of London, has a special place in Queen Mary's affections. Her first public act on becoming Queen was to go there with King George V.

On the death of Queen Alexandra, Queen Mary became its president, and remained so for twenty-five years—until the Government took it over under the Health Services Act. She still refers to it as "My hospital."

One day a little boy in one of the wards said to a nurse: "A lady what works in a Palace is coming to see me tomorow." Next day Queen Mary stood by his bed. "Good afternoon," she said. "I'm the lady what works in a Palace." She liked that phrase, and has often repeated it to friends.

The Queen Mary Maternity Home at Hampstead, is another house of healing in which she has a special interest. Founded at the end of the First World War with money collected by Queen Mary's London Needle-work Guild, as a silver wedding present to the Queen, it was incorporated into "the London" in 1946.

King George, to recuperate after the severe illness of which I wrote at the beginning of this chapter, went to Bognor, which then become Bognor Regis—"King's Bog-nor." And at Bognor Regis is the Princess Mary Memorial Home, named after Queen Mary's mother, and founded years ago to provide holidays for working women from South and East London.

To visit a hospital with Queen Mary is a revelation not only of her sympathy and understanding, but also of the efficiency with which she goes about the inspection of every department, from the operating room to the kitchen. She talks with the doctors, nurses, and patients.

"Don't you think," she says, "that there would be more light in the ward if that wall were painted white?" Or, "These windows seem rather bare. Don't you think that curtains and blinds would make the patients feel more at home?"

Knowing Queen Mary's sympathetic interest in all that concerns the care of the sick, I have often thought what a comfort she must have been to her husband in his own illnesses. Her health had always been better than his.

As a boy, King George V was wiry, active and full of stamina. But even in his early years he suffered often from persistent coughs and colds. Of his later years, Mr. John Gore wrote: "He had often been ill, once at least very gravely, two or three times seriously, slightly ill constantly. . . . He had suffered occasionally from rheumatism and sciatica. . . . Although he gave the appearance of fitness at the beginning of each shooting season, there was probably too severe a contrast between his manner of life in London and in the country."

At the time of his marriage to Queen Mary he had only just recovered from typhoid, which had left him so ill that he was unable to go to the funeral of his elder brother, the Duke of Clarence.

Eight years later, on the night following the accession of his father, King Edward VII, he became seriously ill again, and was in bed for three weeks. So, of all the Royal Family, he was the only one who could not attend the funeral of his grandmother, Queen Victoria.

Royal mourning in those days was a solemn and ceremonious affair.

Nowadays, thanks largely to Queen Mary's example, it has become much less gloomy, without loss of dignity and true feeling. Perhaps it was because she had to wear black so often in her young days that she contracted an active and enduring distaste for it.

It must have been apparent to "Princess May" from the beginning, that in marrying the heir of King Edward VII she had undertaken to care for a man who, in order to carry out his great responsibilities, must keep careful watch on his physical health. The coming of his father to the throne threw additional strain on the young Prince, at a time when his greatest need was rest.

Kingship had come to King Edward VII late in life. He was getting old and tired. The Boer War was still dragging on, and gloom hung over the nation.

It was just then that the Duke and Duchess of York had to face the prospect of leaving their comfortable little home at York Cottage, Sandringham, say farewell to their four lovely children, and set off on the longest and most eventful royal tour in history.

It had been Queen Victoria's idea. Indeed, it was by her command that the Duke and Duchess of York made themselves ready to proceed as her representatives to open the new Commonwealth Parliament at Melbourne in the Spring of 1901.

"Commonwealth?" asked the Queen. "What is that?" Empire she knew, Dominion she knew; but Commonwealth was something that had to be explained to her, wise in statesmanship as she was.

And there was no statesman wise enough or great enough to foresee the day when King George V and Queen Mary would stand together at the head of the British Commonwealth of Nations, something new and fine in the world.

At Tilbury Docks, down the river from London, the Orient liner *Ophir*, painted a dazzling white, was being fitted out for its new duties as bearer of the royal party to the other side of the world.

Queen Mary with King George V during
a visit to Liverpool, 1924.

Central Press Photos Ltd.

Queen Mary with the Duke and Duchess of
York at Balmoral Castle.

Queen Mary in a happy mood
during the Centenary celebrations of University College.

Marcus Adams

Queen Mary and Princess Elizabeth.

At Bognor with King George V, who was
recovering after his serious illness of 1929.

Queen Mary at work on her embroidery
in the grounds of Coppins a few months
after the death of King George V.

The Royal Family on the balcony at Buckingham Palace, after the Coronation of the King and Queen.

A formal portrait of Her Majesty Queen Mary, 1938.

Queen Mary at her writing desk.

Queen Mary holding Baby Prince Charles when he was christened in Buckingham Palace on December 15th, 1948.

P.A.-Reuter

Queen Mary, unhurt after her car crashed, carries out an engagement to have tea in Rosendale Close, West Dulwich.

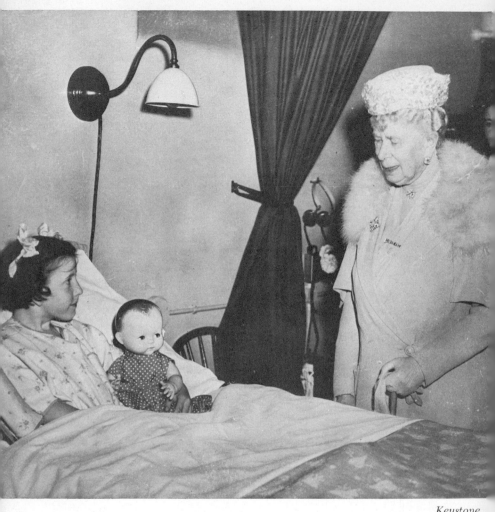

Queen Mary speaking to
nine year old deaf and
dumb Christine Briars at
the London Hospital.

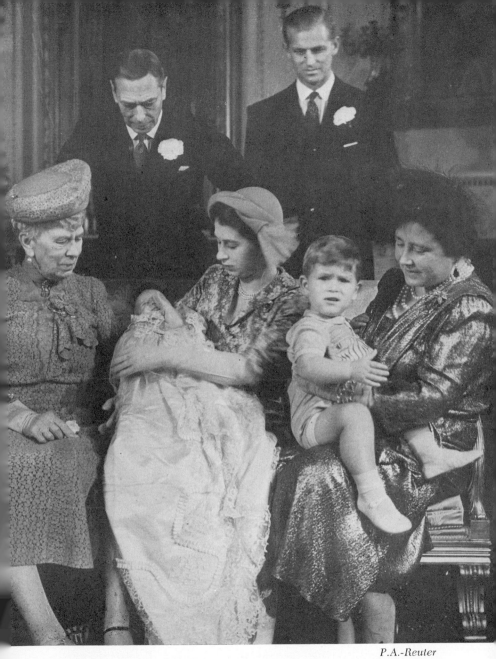

P.A.-Reuter

At the christening of Princess Anne in Buckingham Palace.

Little Prince Charles is determined at getting some
attention, at the christening of his sister, Princess
Anne, much to the amusement of Queen Mary,
Queen Elizabeth and Prince Philip.

Queen Mary with some of the children
at the Pioneer Health Center in Peck-
ham.

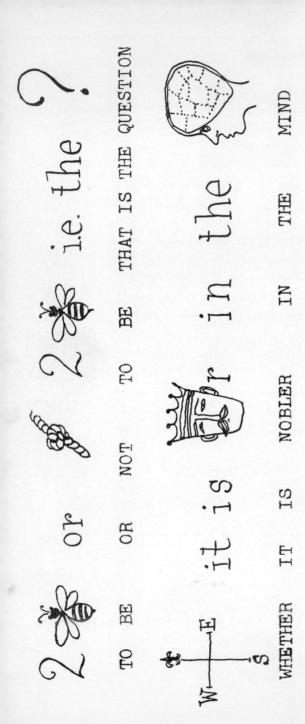

TO BE OR NOT TO BE THAT IS THE QUESTION

WHETHER IT IS NOBLER IN THE MIND

TO SUFFER THE SLINGS AND ARROWS OF OUTRAGEOUS FORTUNE

Woman's Own

At home, the Duke had only a few weeks to learn his own new duties. As a naval officer and as a quiet country gentleman, he had had little opportunity or inclination to study the technique of ceremonial functions.

He put himself as a pupil into the hands of Sir Arthur Bigge, who had been Queen Victoria's private secretary, and the Duke worked day and night to perfect himself in his new tasks.

Perhaps Queen Mary had as much to learn, but learning came more easily to her. No one can have seen her, whether at a great public ceremony or at a private function, or even in the intimacy of her own sitting room, without feeling that she was born with an instinctive gift for correct behavior.

I have heard her described as a consummate actress, but there is far more than acting in the way she carries herself, in the way she moves and speaks and above all in her way of putting others at ease in her presence. It is more than good manners; it is the grand manner itself.

And remember, she has always been shy. Perhaps that shyness is part of the secret of her charm; it is as if she said to herself: "I am a Queen, but I must never forget that I am a human being. And as a human being, I am put on earth to perform certain duties. Since duty has called me to be a Queen, I will be as good a Queen as I can."

I am not presuming to put words into her mouth, but only to attempt to translate into words her actions as we have seen them. There is true humility in Queen Mary.

For eight months the liner *Ophir* was to be the home of the Duke and Duchess of York. For the Duke, there must have been a great thrill in getting back to the sea again, to show his young wife the ports he had known as a naval officer.

She read all the books she could about the places she would visit—Gibraltar, Malta, Port Said, Aden, Ceylon, Singapore, Melbourne, Sydney, Brisbane, Auckland, Wellington, Christchurch, Dunedin, Hobart, Adelaide, Albany, Perth, Mauritius, Durban, Cape Town, Quebec, Halifax, St. John's and across Canada to Victoria.

It was the greatest royal odyssey ever heard of— 45,000 miles, and 33,000 of them by sea.

We know now that there were doubts about the wisdom of having the heir-apparent leave the country at such a time. (Many years later, when King George V's heir, the Prince of Wales, was about to set off for his great voyage in the *Renown,* it was said that Queen Mary, with true motherly feelings, regretted the plan and wished that the journey could be postponed for a year.)

What must have been her feelings, and her husband's at the prospect of leaving their four young children and going off, at the call of duty, to the other side of the world?

The leave-takings were tearful. "Those dreadful farewells," said Queen Mary to a friend, "nearly killed me."

In her cabin (the Duke insisted on her having for herself the nicest quarters in the ship) she arranged the
children's portraits—"a sweet picture of baby Mary . . .
too nice and looks so pretty on my table" and photographs of "David" and "Bertie."

During the recent war, I lived at Windsor Castle with
the Princesses. I occupied the Victoria Tower and
around the walls of my bedroom were delightful water-
colors of the children of King George V and Queen
Mary. The little boys in white sailor suits, looking so
attractive with their fair hair and blue eyes, and their
sister, Princess Mary, so charming in a delightful dress
and a pink rose in her hand—the pink of the rose exactly
matching the pink of her cheeks. No wonder there were
pictures of the children in the Duchess's cabin.

"It is horrible," wrote the Duke, "saying good-bye to
the sweet children."

At a luncheon party in the ship before it sailed he
almost broke down while replying to a toast. "Very
much affected and could hardly speak," he wrote. "The
leave-taking was terrible. I went back with them to the
Yacht when I said good-bye and broke down quite."

Ashore, massed bands played and guns boomed as
the *Ophir* moved out of Portsmouth Harbor. All the
ships in the harbor were gay with flags. But in the
ship, at least some hearts were heavy. "About 5," the
Duke wrote in his cabin, "we passed the *Alberta* quite

close and cheered, a terrible moment. We felt terribly sad, leaving all our darlings."

The crew of the *Ophir* numbered 320, including the laundryman's wife, who was added to the ship's complement because he said that only a woman could handle all the starching and goffering which women's finery demanded in those days.

The list of official personages aboard is too long to give here; it included secretaries, equerries, marine artists, chaplains, ladies-in-waiting and Government representatives.

Also aboard, and a great comfort to the future Queen Mary, was her brother, Prince Alexander of Teck, then an officer of the Seventh Hussars.

Seven years younger than Queen Mary, he is still with us—a tall, handsome, soldierly figure, the husband of Princess Alice, whose residence is in Kensington Palace, a few yards from where I live.

As a young man he was always called by his third name, Frederick, and to Queen Mary, whom he visits often, he is still her beloved "Brother Fred."

It was March when the *Ophir* put to sea, and the weather was bad in the Bay of Biscay. "Unfortunately," the Duchess wrote home, "I am a very bad sailor, and if not actually ill I have a constant headache—a great loss, as being at sea is one's only rest, and it is anything but rest to me." Pelting rain ruined the festivities at Gibraltar, but after that the weather improved.

Then the voyage went more merrily. Soon the *Ophir* (like all the ships the Duke had himself commanded) was a happy ship. He was happiest when he could point out to the Duchess bits of coastline that had long been familiar to him.

Malta, which he knew as well as he knew Sandring‑ham, was dressed in color and light to greet the royal pair.

These receptions gave the Duke and Duchess their first opportunity to test themselves as truly royal per‑sonages, carrying out public duties of the highest im‑portance.

Until then they had been in the background of affairs, and had had little experience of standing on their own feet as public figures. It was indeed a testing time for them. Princess Mary, Duchess of York, was only a name to the people of the far-flung Dominions.

They knew even less about her than the people at home. Photographs of her published in the countries she visited did her far less than justice, and gave no idea of her courtesy, sympathy and charm, which came as a lovely surprise, almost as a revelation, to the people among whom she went.

Everywhere she went they marvelled at her eagerness to see all there was to be seen, her interest in details and her skill in discussing them.

As the voyage continued, gifts accumulated. At Gib‑raltar, a committee of ladies presented her with a beauti‑

ful piece of Barcelona lace, which, to the delight of the crowds, she wore as a mantilla.

At Aden, where the Duchess suffered much from the appalling heat, the Sultan of Lahej came on board to pay his respects, and presented her with a jewelled necklace of native workmanship, receiving in return a photograph of herself. Many such souvenirs came her way in the course of the long voyage.

I am sure that Queen Mary, with her remarkable love of order and method, and her even more wonderful memory, knows the present whereabouts of every one of them.

From Aden the royal couple went to Ceylon, land of spice-laden breezes, where little boys fanned her while the loyal address was read, where she visited a Buddhist monastery and surprised the intelligent young monk who showed her around by the knowledge she had gained about the place beforehand.

Servants in white, crimson and gold, with tortoise-shell combs in their hair waited on the Duke and Duchess. Trained elephants salaamed to them.

At Singapore, the four Malayan Sultans were presented to them, and they rode in rickshaws through the Chinese quarter. And after that, on the voyage to Melbourne, our Queen Mary became the first British Princess to cross the Equator.

Indeed, the Duke and Duchess were making a new path in history all the way. They saw for the first time, in the cities, lands, and peoples of Australia, New Zealand and Canada, what the British Empire really meant. They performed far more than the great mission on which they had embarked; they were to bring home far more than souvenirs.

I have seen some of the pictures that were taken on that journey of banquets, receptions and reviews of troops. One I like best shows the young Duchess picnicking in the Australian Bush, sitting on an upturned paraffin tin, with the Duke perched uncomfortably on an upturned log.

She was in mourning, of course, for most of the time, and that raised the question of etiquette for the ladies of the Dominions. But sometimes etiquette went overboard, as, for example, when Sydney undergraduates sang:

> *And when he at last appears,*
> *The welkin we shall rouse,*
> *By giving the Jook three cheers,*
> *And three for his charming spouse;*
> *And every undergrad*
> *With a throat to call his own,*
> *Will not overlook the Dad*
> *Who is minding the kids at home.*

Thoughts of the children at home were often in their minds. The Duke wrote to his mother. "You will have read the accounts in the papers of our doings here and at Brisbane. We have certainly had a very busy time, we have tried our best to be civil to and please everyone.

"Darling May is of the greatest possible help to me and works very hard. I don't think I could have done all this without her. Everybody admires her very much, which is very pleasing to me. I hope you are as proud of your daughter-in-law as I am of my wife.

"So glad to hear that the sweet children are well and flourishing and that you have had them with you at Sandringham; but I think it a pity that Bricka did not go, as David really ought to do a few lessons each day; he is 7 years old already."

And at last, after the months of absence, they came home to their children, who stood with King Edward VII and Queen Alexandra on the deck of the royal yacht to welcome them.

Four days later, in their newly conferred dignity of Prince and Princess of Wales, they drove through London to receive the city's official welcome. From the carriage they caught sight of Marlborough House, their new home, where Queen Mary still lives.

She and her husband had come through a long and exhausting ordeal and had done great work for Britain and the Empire. It is not too much to say that they had inaugurated a new era. They had brought home a new conception of Empire—brought home to the British people the true meaning of Kipling's question, "What do they know of England, who only England know?" In a speech at the Guildhall soon after his return, the new Prince of Wales electrified his hearers by declaring, "The Old Country must wake up!"

To his father, King Edward VII, he wrote, with humble heart: "It makes me very happy to know that you are pleased with the way that May and I carried out the very important mission which you entrusted to us." us."

Always "May and I!"

```
┌─────────────────────────┐
│                         │
│                         │
│     PART NINE           │
│                         │
│                         │
└─────────────────────────┘
```

Long ago, when Queen Mary was "Princess May," people called her "The Children's Princess," because she always seemed happiest when she had children around her. Now, for forty years, she has been "The Children's Queen."

Surely her two baby great-grandchildren are a source of joy to her. No one can have witnessed her delight in the company of the Little Princesses, when I used to take them to Marlborough House to see her, without realizing that she loves children for their own sake.

"Grannie's Birthday" was always a great occasion for them, as it still is now that they are grown up.

Usually their mother took them to Marlborough House to see their Grannie on her birthday, but once I had that enjoyable duty. It was while King George VI and Queen Elizabeth were making their historic visit to Canada and the United States, just before the outbreak of the 1939–1945 War.

Queen Mary was in bed with a slight chill, and in a lovely bed-jacket of pink satin, she looked as regal as ever.

I remember thinking: "Why, this is a regular Royal levee, in the true sense. Kings used to receive their courtiers in bed; it was a great honor for them." And I realized that I too was greatly honored.

The Queen was sitting up to greet her grandchildren with a smile. At her back was a head pillow of pink satin and lace, like the one she always uses when she travels. It was from her that I learned the habit of using a head pillow; it rests the neck and is a great comfort.

On the way to Marlborough House in the car, Princess Elizabeth and Princess Margaret held in their hands little Victorian posies—tight bunches of flowers in frilled paper holders. These they presented to Grannie, wishing her a happy birthday and kissing her on the cheek. It was easy to see how pleased she was. The posies were placed in vases beside her bed, where she could look at them.

On the bedside tables were all sorts of quaint and pretty things—fans, china ornaments, gilt, enameled and lacquered boxes and knick-knacks.

"See how many friends I have!" said Queen Mary, and explained that many of these presents had come from people who were strangers to her only because they did not give their names. Then she said to the Princesses, "Would you like to choose something for yourselves?"

Like all nicely brought up children, they said, both together, "Oh, Grannie! We really couldn't." But after a little persuasion, of course they found that they could, and they took two little china animals. It was my turn next, and I received a lovely painted fan of French workmanship, which, as you may be sure, I still treasure.

Also beside the bed was a heap of letters, most of which, like the presents, were from people not personally known to Queen Mary, but to her, nevertheless, "my dear friends." The children and I were allowed to read a few of the letters. Some, on thick notepaper, were from people whose names and titles they knew, but I remember one, written in blue crayon on a ruled page from a child's exercise book; it began, "Dear Queen Mary." The children loved that.

"It's nearly as tidy as one of your letters," said Princess Elizabeth to Princess Margaret. And I think this is a good place for me to tell you of a schoolroom trick Princess Margaret invented when she was small.

Queen Mary was eager that the Princesses should learn poetry by heart, and as much of it as possible. To-day this is scorned by some of the modern educationalists. They say that people grow up hating the poems they were made to learn at school. On the other hand, there is a great deal to be said for Queen Mary's insistence on learning poetry by heart. There can be no doubt that it does sharpen the memory and stimulate the mind, besides equipping one with a stock of useful quotations and their sources.

Princess Elizabeth was an extraordinarily quick learner, and took a very short time indeed to become word-perfect; I am sure that she could recite Tennyson's "Ulysses" from memory to-day. But Princess Margaret, much to Queen Mary's amusement, went about learning poetry in a different way. For example, to learn "Hamlet's" "To be, or not to be" soliloquy, she drew a series of rebuses. The sketch shown is not her actual drawing, but it will give you the idea. Princess Margaret worked out that method for herself, and so got many long passages from Shakespeare by heart.

Many of the most characteristic pictures of Queen Mary show her with children, and they are always her happiest pictures.

Her best jokes, revealing a sense of humor that no one who saw her only on State occasions would suspect, concern the antics of small children. When they come hesitatingly to make a presentation to her, she stoops to greet them—and to conquer with a smile. I have seen her keeping quite solemn when some public function was going on, and then break into smiles when a child made an awkward curtsy, took panic at the last moment and hid his face in his mother's skirt.

They were smiles of reassurance, encouragement, comfort and sympathy—as if Queen Mary longed to step out of her part and gather the child in her own arms.

On one such occasion I heard a woman say, "Don't the children love her!" And another replied. "She understands them, you see. She's had six of her own, remember." Who could forget? Queen Mary's children were growing up in the years when she and her husband had to leave them at home and make the great Empire tour which was the real inauguration of their public career.

From then on, as Prince and Princess of Wales and then as King and Queen, public duties called them often from the family circle.

For example, there was the State visit to Vienna, where Queen Mary's eldest brother, who was Military Attaché there, "clasped her round the waist in her descent from the train and kissed her in truly British fashion."

In a dress of bright heliotrope, Princess Mary was saluted by the Viennese crowds as *"Die Schöne Prinzessin May."* The Emperor asked her to open a Grand Ball at Hofburg, when she danced into the small hours of the morning.

Their third son, the late Duke of Kent, was born near the end of the busy year which saw more State visits and also King Edward VII's coronation.

After that, his father had much less time than he

would have liked to spend with the children, but his mother continued to be with them for whole months on end.

When the sixth child, the short-lived Prince John, was born at Sandringham, his father went there to await the birth, and told his diary how he enjoyed "the delight of peace and quiet after London."

"Once more," writes Mr. John Gore, "the Prince fell into the routine he had made customary following the births of all his younger children at the Cottage. He gave the Princess her breakfast at nine o'clock each morning and spent much available time reading to her during the day. The Princess made her usual rapid recovery."

And then there were only a few busy, hurrying months before the Prince and Princess of Wales had to be off again—to India, where they visited nearly every State, met all the Princes and made a great round of banquets, speeches, interviews and journeys.

"The unadvertised and unplanned contacts made by the Prince and Princess," says Sir Walter Lawrence, who had charge of the program, "played quite as important a part in the general success as did their conduct of the listed functions. . . .

"I was greatly impressed by their kindness and patience and by the keen interest they took in everything Indian. We prepared a small library of books on Indian subjects. I knew that the Princess read them, and the Prince knew most of the important passages."

One of the most pleasing public duties of the Princess in India was the opening of the Victoria Zenana Hospital for women at Hyderabad. Until that time women's welfare, especially in the matter of childbirth, had been little considered.

"In this hospital," wrote a correspondent, "there will be space for sixty patients, half of them maternity cases, with modern facilities for training Indian nurses and midwives.

"Only those acquainted with the East can appreciate the priceless value of the work the Princess advanced by her active participation in the ceremony at Hyderabad."

It was work after her own heart, and so were the many Purdah parties she attended, where women only, unveiled, met and talked behind the high walls which shut them off from the world of men.

At a lavishly colorful entertainment in Bombay Town Hall, with the walls hung with rich embroideries and shawls and the floors covered with silk Persian carpets, the Princess sat on a golden throne and was fanned by women in gorgeous raiment swinging large punkahs of gold woven on crimson.

A sugar sweet was waved round her head three times, so that her life would be filled with sweetness. A lamp resting on a tray was passed round her, with the prayer that her path might always be bright. Maidens with nets of white flowers resting in their dark hair cast gold and silver at the feet of the Princess to remind her that "the poor are always with us." Then an Indian lady threw over her a rainbow-colored shower of real pearls.

Pleasures and palaces! And all the time, as we know by the Prince's diary, their hearts were at home with their children. The parting had been even harder than the first one, because most of them were now old enough to feel the separation.

Throughout the tour the Princess gathered specimens of minerals, timbers, and other interesting things—all carefully collected and catalogued—so that the young Princes and their sister could be shown something of the resources of India.

On the eve of her departure she wrote: "We are leaving India, where we have spent four and a half happy months, with intense regret. But how I am looking forward to seeing the dear children!"

Queen Victoria had once said: "There is nothing worse or more destructive than treating young people at a very early age as if they were quite independent and grown-up. This especially applies to Royalty. The longer one can keep them as children the better it is." She also believed that "a boy of fifteen and a half is actually like a girl of twelve."

Certainly Queen Mary's children were given as happy a childhood as was possible in a royal household. Stories are told that may suggest that they were overdisciplined. For example, if one of them came down late for a meal he was not allowed to sit at table, but had to eat from a tray in his own apartments. But that was only a lesson in punctuality, and punctuality is second nature to Queen Mary, who cannot bear that anyone should be kept waiting for her.

The Princes and their sister were brought up simply, at the White Lodge, Frogmore and Sandringham House, away from the glitter of the court.

In the country, they lived largely an outdoor life, riding, walking, bicycling and often going on picnics organized by their mother. They played at soldiers, with Princess Mary (now the Princess Royal) in a white frock, short socks, buttoned boots, and sailor hat, drilling her brothers on the lawn.

But fun and games were never allowed to interfere with the children's lessons. Queen Mary personally superintended the education of her daughter and the younger Princes. Princess Mary, always under the one governess, went to classes with other girls, and so made friends of her own age.

In London, Queen Mary took her children to see the Tower, the National Gallery and other places, just as, years later, she took Princess Elizabeth and Princess Margaret on those memorable Monday afternoons that I have described. Queen Mary's children learned to swim at the Bath Club, where, later, Princess Elizabeth and Princess Margaret also learned to swim.

Shopping expeditions, too, were pleasures that no other royal children had ever been able to enjoy. Queen Mary, as Princess of Wales, broke with the old tradition of Queen Victoria and Queen Alexandra, who never went to the shops but had the goods sent to them for inspection at the Palace.

Queen Mary often did her own shopping—usually in the big Kensington stores—and took her children with her. The toy departments at Christmas time were their special delight. They were given just so much money to spend, and when that was done, no more toys. And they knew that many of their used toys would be sent to the homes of poor people.

And once, for Prince Edward and Prince Albert (the future King George VI), there was a day of days—an outing such as no Royal Princes before them could ever have had.

They went to the White City, the great exhibition at Shepherd's Bush, which their parents had officially opened a few weeks before.

Pouring rain had marred the opening, at which the Prince of Wales wore an Admiral's uniform and the Princess a heliotrope coat and skirt, white ostrich boa and lace-crowned toque. The grounds were a sea of mud.

The boy Princes had better weather for their expedition. With their tutor, Mr. Hansell, they queued up to pay their shillings for admission, and again for sixpennyworth of the Scenic Railway.

They saw everything and tried everything—the Witching Waves, the Helter-Skelter, the Johnstown Flood, and the Switchback. They bought toffee, and ate it as they rode. They posted picture postcards. No boys from a London slum could have enjoyed an outing more—or as much, for this was a taste of the sort of freedom that Princes seldom get.

They went to the White City again before the summer was over, and then they had to go back to school —to the Royal Naval College at Osborne, where both were to become cadets.

How close they were as boys, how alike was their upbringing, and yet how different their natures and their destinies proved to be! Some people say now that Prince Edward was spoiled. If so, it was not by his parents. Good-looking, full of charm, he was bound to have a great fuss made of him wherever he went. He was King Edward's favorite grandson, perhaps because the King saw in him a chip off the old block. On his tenth birthday the King gave him a party at Buckingham Palace, and laughed to see the dignity with which the boy received his guests. "Infernally bumptious," said the King.

Once, King Edward asked the Prince what he had been reading, and the reply was: "The story of Perkin Warbeck, who pretended to be of royal descent but really was born of respectable parents."

Only her high position sets Queen Mary apart from

the multitude of British mothers. In all other respects she is one of them and one with them. As the mother of four boys who served the nation in war, she has shared the griefs and anxieties of her countrywomen.

When the First World War began her eldest son, Prince Edward, was just twenty, and the next, Prince Albert (who is now King George VI) was eighteen and a half.

Prince Albert, who was recovering from an appendicitis operation, went, as soon as he was fit, into active service with the Royal Navy, to fight as a sub-lieutenant in the fore turret of the *Collingwood*. In the *Collingwood's* hot duel with the *Derfflinger*, the *Collingwood* was hit. The Prince was at his 12-inch gun throughout the action. For his coolness and gallantry he was mentioned in Despatches.

But, of course, Prince Edward, as heir to the throne, was more in the public eye. He begged to be allowed to go to the front at once. "What does it matter if I am shot?" he asked. "I have three brothers."

After the first battle of Ypres he was allowed to go, and soon he was under fire, wading through mud and alarming the senior officers who felt responsible for his life.

Sir Phillip Gibbs, the famous war correspondent, saw him there, and wrote: "Who was that young officer, a mere boy, who came toiling up through the slime and mud?" He turned, and saw that he was Edward, Prince of Wales. All Britain was proud of him as the Prince of Wales, but Queen Mary had also a mother's pride.

Prince Henry, Duke of Gloucester, destined also to be a soldier, was at that time a fag at Eton. So was Leopold, then Crown Prince of Belgium. All that now seems long ago, for so much has happened since, but I am sure that it is still vivid in Queen Mary's memory.

Closer to our own time is the short but gallantly tragic part played by her third son, Prince George, Duke of Kent, in the Second Great War.

His death in an air crash on active service shocked the nation, but also brought home to us, with pride, the realization that the Royal Family were not only bearing their own heavy responsibilities, but also were sharing our dangers.

We all remembered the gladness with which the British people had taken the Duke of Kent's bride, the beautiful Princess Marina, to their hearts. When her husband was killed, Queen Mary's first thought was to comfort the Duchess and her children.

In the Princess Royal, Queen Mary has a devoted daughter and loving companion. When King George V died, the Princess comforted her mother with tender care and solicitude, staying by her side. And later, when the Princess's own husband, Lord Harewood, died, Queen Mary in her turn did everything in her power to quiet the grief and distress of her daughter by always being at hand, with love and understanding.

Queen Mary and her daughter were brought together by another bond of grief during the last war, when the Princess's son, who was then Lord Lascelles, was wounded and taken prisoner. The news came from a foreign radio station.

After that there was silence. For a long time nothing was known of what had happened to him. Anxiety was felt everywhere; it brought Queen Mary and the Princess Royal more than ever into the hearts of all women whose sons, husbands or brothers were prisoners of war

When her sons married, Queen Mary welcomed their wives into the bosom of the Royal Family. To her daughters-in-law, she is a fountain-head of wisdom and loving counsel, and they never hesitate to go to her for advice and sympathy.

There are probably many women who think it must be quite an ordeal for the future wife of a son of Queen Mary to meet such a regal personage for the first time. It is not so. I have often seen Queen Mary with her daughters-in-law. No one else in all the world could have made them feel so much at home—almost as if they were Queen Mary's own daughters—in so short a time.

Think also of the deep happiness of Queen Mary with the Duke of York's choice—The Lady Elizabeth Bowes-Lyon, our present gracious and lovely Queen. What comfort and happiness that marriage must have brought to Queen Mary! Although he was not the heir to the throne, he was the first of her sons to take a wife, and perhaps there was an omen in that. It was a real love match, and all rejoiced in it.

It has brought them two lovely daughters, one of whom, the heir-apparent, has married the man of her choice and given Queen Mary two beautiful great grandchildren.

We know that Queen Mary is happiest when she has children around her. What comfort it must be to her to know that she is surrounded by nine grandchildren, all growing up loving her and thinking of her as a very great lady!

PART TEN

"The King's life is moving peacefully to its close."

Like the sad tolling of a bell, hour after hour, the solemn message went out to the world. It was indeed a passing-bell, calling millions to prayer.

In British cities, towns and villages, men and women knelt in the streets. Mariners at sea, cow-hands on Canadian ranches, dwellers at wayside stations in the Australian Bush, heard the call with sorrow in their hearts. And in their prayers they remembered Queen Mary.

Sitting by her husband's bedside in the red-carpeted room at Sandringham, watching her husband sleep, Queen Mary had need of all the sympathy that flowed towards her. It was not the first time that King George V had been near death. Seven years before, he had been gravely ill for six months. The nation had celebrated his recovery at a Thanksgiving Service in Westminster Abbey.

"Fancy a Thanksgiving Service with a hole in your back," he said, with a grim smile, to Lord Dawson, his physician; and there had to be another operation before he could resume his work.

But this last time there was to be no Thanksgiving Service and no resumption of work. At five minutes before midnight, on January 20th, 1936, he laid down his heavy burden. With him when he died were the Prince of Wales, the Duke of York, the Princess Royal and the Duke and Duchess of Kent.

Outside the wind howled. One of the worst storms of winter was sweeping the country; it is a background of a picture that is fixed forever in the memories of millions.

In countless homes, after the radio had no more to say, families stayed up far into the morning hours to talk and try to realize the meaning of what had happened to all of us.

King George V had never quite been able to realize how deeply he had come into the hearts of the people. His last Christmas broadcast, only a few days before, was still fresh in their minds. Many could repeat the actual closing words:

"I send to you all, and not least to the children who may be listening to me, my truest Christmas wishes, and those of my dear wife, my children and grand-children who are with me to-day. I add a heartfelt prayer that, wherever you may be, God may bless and keep you always."

Fresh in their minds, too, was the Jubilee speech that had come to them only a few months before. If not the words, they recalled how his voice almost broke near the end, when he spoke of Queen Mary. So, we said to one another, he too feels what everyone was feeling.

Many years before, after a particularly fulsome ad-dress had been presented to him, he had said to a secre-tary: "It's extraordinary; for I'm quite an ordinary sort of fellow." And on Jubilee Night, after the great parade and demonstration of the people's affection, he said: "Do they really think so much of me?" His modesty for-bade him to believe it, but it was true, and we never saw the truth more clearly than on the night he died.

What of Queen Mary now? I pondered that question in my snowbound home in Dunfermline, where I had gone for Christmas. Next day the wires were down, and I could not reply to the telegram from the Duchess of York asking me to return as soon as possible to the Royal Lodge, Windsor Great Park, where the Princesses were; so, as soon as I could gather some black clothes together, I set off on the long, cold, miserable journey.

As I write, that strange, unreal train ride, which took all day, comes back to my mind—the quiet railway sta-tions we stopped at on the way South were almost empty, as if the people felt that they ought not to be going about their ordinary affairs at such a time. The whole white land seemed to be hushed. People whispered if they had to speak at all. It was as if the heart of the Empire stood still.

Just as happens in family life, when our near and dear ones leave us, we suddenly realize, perhaps for the first time, how much they have meant to us and how desolate we are without them, so, I felt, the people of Britain were realizing how much they would miss their King.

The same hush was on the Royal Lodge—no more intense, but with a special poignancy.

I found Princess Elizabeth waiting for me, the Duchess having gone to London and the Duke to Sandringham. Princess Elizabeth was silent and sad, but Princess Margaret, too young to understand, laughed and played. The three of us sat at a low table which stretched the whole length of one wall of the schoolroom, and played with the Princesses' model farm until Princess Margaret went off to her bath and bed, to be followed soon after by Princess Elizabeth.

In "The Little Princesses" I have told how I took Princess Elizabeth to London for the funeral, and left her, a pathetic little figure in black coat and beret and short white socks, with her mother at Paddington station, while the King's Pipers played "The Flowers of the Forest," and the King, followed by his own kinfolk, set off on his last journey, to be buried at Windsor.

When the train had left the station, I noticed for the first time that my right hand, which Princess Elizabeth had clutched tightly while we waited, was tingling with "pins and needles," as if some of the little girl's pent-up emotion had escaped to me.

How strange it seemed, in the months that followed, for us to have a new King and no Queen to share his throne. The British people have loved their Queens and Princesses. Two of our greatest monarchs were Queens in their own right, as Princess Elizabeth, by the grace of God, one day will be. Without a Queen Consort, there seemed a curious emptiness in the land.

But what a consolation it was for us, in the months before King George VI came to the throne, to have Queen Mary with us—Consort no longer, "The Queen Mother" by official designation, but still the Queen Mary the nation had loved and honored for twenty-six years.

"Queen Mary," she was called in the Court Circular, in a message thanking the people for the sympathy at the ending of her "forty-two years of happy married life"; and Queen Mary she will always be to us all.

To face widowhood after a long, happy and busy married life is a stern ordeal for any woman. Her whole way of living must change.

For a Queen, the changes are sweeping and abrupt. For Queen Mary, apart from the loss of a life's com-

panionship, it was far more than the move from Buckingham Palace to Marlborough House. At once she had
to step down, to adjust herself to her new position, to
become an onlooker instead of a chief figure on occasions of State, to give place to her son.

If she had any misgivings about King Edward VIII
she did not utter them or show them, but went on as
the loving mother she had always been, and as a duti-
ful subject.

Over and over again in this series of articles, I have
shown how her devotion to duty has always governed
her ways, and this was never more apparent than in
the dignity and wisdom with which she took up the
burden of widowhood. As she laid down her State
duties, she embarked at once on a new course of service.

Many a wife, bereft of her husband, retreats into a
life of perpetual gloom, brooding disconsolately over
such things as her husband's personal belongings, so
embarrassing to her friends.

Queen Victoria, after the Prince Consort's death, almost buried herself alive for many years. Queen Mary
was old enough to remember that time. But when her
husband died, instead of isolating herself in the retirement to which her years would have entitled her, she
dedicated her life anew to the nation and took up new
interests, keeping the memory of King George V clearly
before us by carrying on his great tradition of service to
the people.

We often hear people—usually men—talk about "retiring" from business. Working women, it seems, are expected to keep on until they drop, sometimes in the course of their duties as housekeepers to men often younger than themselves.

Some men look forward eagerly to a few years of ease and freedom from work. Others are afraid that they will be bored, and wonder what games to learn to pass the time. Doctors warn them that to cut themselves off too suddenly from the interests of a lifetime may be dangerous; and point to the vital statistics, which certainly do prove that old people are more likely to die in their beds than young people.

If ever a woman was entitled to retire when her big job came to an end, Queen Mary was. She was long past the age when most men cease work. But she has never retired, and I am sure that she has no intention of ever doing so.

That is not mind-reading, but reading the facts and actions that speak for themselves. We know that she herself has said, "I have never been bored in my life." As a young Princess she startled statesmen and economists by asking them searching questions about wages and industrial conditions. All her life she has been interested in the way the people live, in hospital work, and, above all, in child welfare. While she was Queen Consort she had to be content, most of the time, to learn by reading.

State functions took up so much of her time that she was unable often to go about and see for herself what was going on in the streets, in the shops, in factories, and in the people's homes, much as she would have liked to do so. But as Queen Mother, when the period of mourning was over and the throne was secure, she seized her opportunities to meet people. "I admire people who do things," she once said, and those were the people she sought.

There is a clue to her interests in her choice of The Lady Cynthia Colville as one of her ladies-in-waiting, for Lady Cynthia spends much of her time, when not in-waiting, as a magistrate at the London Juvenile Court. A most distinguished-looking woman, and a superb conversationalist, full of wit, she studies at first hand the social problems of young people. Not long ago, Lady Cynthia's son, Mr. John Colville, told me laughingly that discomfort meant little to his mother, who at that time was touring France, third-class.

In her, Queen Mary has a lady-in-waiting who is in close touch with all that is happening around us. I should not be surprised to learn that it was she who told Queen Mary about "Pick-Up Girl," the problem play that Queen Mary went to see because she had heard that it was about children who were led astray. Child delinquency is a subject that interests her greatly, and she would be able to hear much about it from Lady Cynthia.

Queen Mary is not outwardly emotional, and she can view conditions, however sordid or harrowing, with calm judgment, her chief concern undoubtedly being how to improve the conditions. I have had many talks with Queen Mary and Lady Cynthia about social and industrial problems, and the question has always been, "Do you think Princess Elizabeth realizes this, and wouldn't it be a good idea for her to see for herself?"

While King George V and Queen Mary were at Buckingham Palace, what little theater-going she did had to be ceremonial. It was not just a matter of telephoning for seats and dropping in casually. Our present King and Queen have been known to do that, on the Queen's birthday, for example, when the King wanted to give her a surprise. But King George V found it easier to stick to the old rules than to make new ones. Not that he was forbiddingly stiff.

Of a visit to Vienna as a young man, he wrote in his diary: "My goodness, this court is stiff. Everyone is afraid of the Emperor." And at the end of a busy season, when he was King, he wrote: "Last Court function this season, thank goodness." And stiffness is the last word I should apply to Queen Mary. Graciousness is the right word. She knows how to unbend.

Members of her household have told me how heartily she threw herself into acting charades at the Christmas family gatherings at Sandringham. "She can be really funny," I was told. "She can hold her own in all the antics that charades call for."

As I have said, Queen Mary was always interested in acting, and in serious plays, and had friends among the famous actors of her young days. Indeed, I have been told that she herself took part in several private amateur performances of popular plays at Windsor and acquitted herself well.

She was delighted when the little Princesses were taken to Christmas pantomimes by their parents, and more delighted still when they acted in private pantomimes of their own at Windsor. But their assurance puzzled her—so modern, so different from girls of her own day. "I can't understand how they do everything so easily," she said to me once, talking of one of those war-time performances of theirs.

King George V did not share his wife's interests in the serious theater. Shakespeare, he said, was "sad stuff." He went to see *King Lear,* and "didn't think much of it."

Queen Mary's love of the theater, although she could not always indulge in it freely, has stayed with her all her life. I am sure that she has saved the program of every play she ever saw—and not only the elaborately printed programs that were specially made for the official royal visits to the theater, but also the ordinary sixpenny program that most people throw away after the show. She keeps other play-going souvenirs too.

The story of one of these souvenirs is another illustration of her remarkable memory as well as her thoughtfulness. Not long ago she went to see *The School for Scandal* at the New Theater. It was on the eve of the investiture of the manager, Sir Bronson Albery, as a Knight. In the interval she sent for him.

"I should like to return this to you," she said, producing a gold pencil. She smiled at the puzzled look on Sir Bronson's face. Return? He had no recollection of lending or giving a pencil to Queen Mary.

"It was your mother's," she said, "and I should like you to have it now."

Sir Bronson's mother was Mary Moore, who had been a famous actress when Queen Mary was Princess May. Mary Moore's husband, James Albery, was the dramatist whose *Two Roses* gave Sir Henry Irving his first big success. Fifty-eight years ago Mary Moore met Princess May in Switzerland and gave her the pencil.

Fifty-eight years! That was just before Princess May's wedding to Prince George. And she remembered a pencil, and had treasured it, and finally could make that gracious use of it!

What a host of memories are stored in her mind! And what tales she could tell, of love, of war, of happiness, of sorrows, of splendid occasions and of people great and small, if ever she sat down to write her own memoirs.

For the first few months after the death of King

George V she still had to be so wrapped up in great affairs that she was unable to set about the new round of activities that she must have planned for herself.

There was the part she had to play in the dramatic weeks leading up to King Edward VIII's abdication. It was a mother's part, but national affairs were at stake. There was the beginning of the new reign, the preparations for the Coronation and the great event itself. There was the getting ready of Marlborough House, and Queen Mary's moving there.

It was at Marlborough House that I really came to know Queen Mary. Of course I had seen her often, and talked with her, at Buckingham Palace and Windsor Castle; but there she was the Queen of England, always gracious, always charming, always kind, but always the Queen. I revered her.

At Marlborough House, I saw her for the first time as a woman in her own home. It was there, in the historic house where she had been taken as a child to meet "the Wales children," that I listened to her wisdom while the silver kettle came to the boil over the spirit lamp and she made tea.

It was there that she worked at her embroidery while a lady-in-waiting read to her—not because Queen Mary dislikes reading but because for her it was one good way of doing two things at once.

And it was from Marlborough House that she used to set out for those Monday afternoon excursions to museums, art galleries, and historic buildings, to show the little Princesses how things were made and how other people lived and had lived.

And from Queen Mary I learned to see what a lovely thing it was to have grandchildren, and what a consolation in widowhood.

After the shock of bereavement, widowhood brought to Queen Mary no respite from the cares of State, or time to adjust herself to a new way of living, but problems as great as any Queen in history had ever had to face. Instead of being given leisure to plan in tranquillity her future round of activities, she found herself suddenly confronted by a crisis that was to test and prove the strength of the ties between her own family and the British people.

Some people had felt, even while the old King was alive, that the Prince of Wales was not taking the path that some of his advisers would have chosen, and that his birth and upbringing had marked out for him. Although British newspapers had carefully and loyally refrained from coupling the names of the Prince and Mrs. Wallis Simpson, the foreign Press, particularly in America, was busy with speculation, hints, and wild surmise.

There was, of course, no censorship of British newspapers, but only the voluntary, traditional agreement among them to print nothing until it was known to be true. And much that was printed abroad at the time went far beyond the truth. Royalty was not fair game for gossip, because Royalty could not answer back. I like to think now that King George V was mercifully spared any knowledge of these rumors, for we knew how sternly he always had deprecated even the harmless, democratic lapses from strict formality that the Prince had permitted, encouraged, and enjoyed on his visits to Canada and the United States. The coming crisis was a far more serious affair.

Whether or not King George V had heard of these rumors which began to spread in the last autumn of his life, I feel sure that Queen Mary was aware of them. All of us knew something of what was going on, and Queen Mary, with her quick perception, her womanly intuition, and her love for all her family, must have been one of the first to sense it. And we know that the Prince of Wales was close to his mother and always ready to confide in her.

So, instead of being able, with a calm mind, to go about the business of moving from Buckingham Palace to Marlborough House—to well-earned ease in retirement—Queen Mary had to continue to play an important part in great affairs. And that her part in these affairs was private, not public, must have made the burden the more difficult to bear.

It has often been said that the Prince of Wales was her favorite son, and that she had placed all her hopes in him. My own view is that it was Queen Mary's high sense of duty, as Queen and Queen Mother, which transcended her personal feelings, her family attachments, and upheld her through the months of crisis.

The Prince of Wales was always a favorite of Princess Elizabeth and Princess Margaret. The Prince Charming whom the multitudes acclaimed was always the beloved Uncle David to his nieces. Elsewhere I have told how, when his name first became linked with that of Mrs. Simpson, I tried to explain the circumstances to them in words that they would understand. Perhaps the explanation helped to prepare them for the sudden change in their own lives.

But, for Queen Mary, there was no consolation. The greatest share of understanding had to come from her. She, so recently bereaved, was the one person to whom all her family had to turn for guidance and support.

I had met Mrs. Simpson first as a visitor to the Royal Lodge, Windsor, where she came to tea with the new King and two or three of his friends. I am bound to say that I found her smart, attractive, friendly and even fascinating. She was also perfectly poised.

I remember her drawing King Edward to a window and suggesting how the view could be improved by moving some trees and taking away part of the hill. Though the Duke and Duchess of York behaved with quiet and charming dignity, there was an awkwardness in the atmosphere. I was glad when the Duchess asked me to take the children for a walk in the woods.

"Crawfie," asked Lilibet as soon as we were away from the house, "Who is she?"

Somehow I managed to evade the question. It was not until the crisis was all over that I could explain to Lilibet that Uncle David had fallen in love with someone Britain could not accept as Queen, because she had been married before, and her husband was still living. Meanwhile both children seemed to sense that something was amiss. Conversations would be broken off as we entered a room. Once the children were asked to go over to Fort Belvedere, the new King's country house, not far from the Royal Lodge, for tea. It was difficult to explain to them why they could not go.

King Edward must often have talked with his mother about Mrs. Simpson before that day in October, 1936, when he decided to bring matters to a head at an audience he granted to Prime Minister Baldwin. And it was to Queen Mary that Mr. Baldwin went, over and over again, during the swift, delicate negotiations that followed. He drove straight from Cabinet meetings to Marlborough House to seek guidance from her store of wise experience, and inspiration from the love she bore her children.

And King Edward went straight from his conferences with Mr. Baldwin to talk with his mother, who was the first to know that he had made up his mind to marry Mrs. Simpson, come what may. That he told her before he told the Prime Minister or anyone else was revealed by Mr. Baldwin in his historic address to the House of Commons.

King Edward spent the last afternoon of his reign with his mother, who drove over to Fort Belvedere to talk with him. The talk became a family conference as it was joined later by the Duke of York and the Duke of Kent.

The next day, Queen Mary, in unaccustomed black, drove to 145 Piccadilly, to spend the afternoon with her daughter-in-law, the Duchess of York, soon to be Queen. While the two women talked, the news of the King's fateful decision was given to the hushed House of Commons, and so to the world.

The same evening Queen Mary drove to the Royal Lodge, Windsor, to join all her sons at a sad farewell party given by the new King, George VI, to his brother, Prince Edward. After dinner they all talked for a while, and then the abdicating King left, alone, for Windsor Castle to make the broadcast speech which brought sadness to the nation's hearts and tears to the nation's eyes.

At long last I am able to say a few words of my own. I have never wanted to withhold anything, but until now, it has not been constitutionally possible for me to speak. A few hours ago I discharged my last duty as King and Emperor, and now that I have been succeeded by my brother, the Duke of York, my first words must be to declare my allegiance to him. This I do with all my heart. You all know the reasons which have impelled

*me to renounce the Throne, but I want you to under-
stand that in making up my mind I did not forget the
country or the Empire, which as Prince of Wales and
lately as King I have for twenty-five years tried to serve.
But you must believe me when I tell you that I have
found it impossible to carry the heavy burden of responsibility, and to discharge my duties as King as I
would wish to do without the help and support of the
woman I love. And I want you to know that the decision
I have made has been mine and mine alone. This was
a thing I had to judge entirely for myself.*

*The other person most nearly concerned has tried up
to the last to persuade me to take a different course.
I have made this, the most serious decision of my life,
only upon a single thought—of what would in the end be
best for all.*

*This decision has been made less difficult to me by the
knowledge that my brother, with his long training in the
public affairs of this country, and with his fine qualities,
will be able to take my place forthwith without interrup-
tion or injury to the life and progress of the Empire. And
he has one matchless blessing, enjoyed by so many of
you, and not bestowed on me, a happy home with his
wife and children.*

*During these hard days I have been comforted by Her
Majesty, my mother, and by my family.*

*The Ministers of the Crown and in particular Mr.
Baldwin have always treated me with full considera-*

tion. There has never been any constitutional difference between me and them and between me and Parliament. Bred in the Constitution traditions by my father, I should never have allowed any such issue to arise.

Ever since I was Prince of Wales, and later on when I occupied the Throne, I have been treated with the greatest kindness by all classes of people, wherever I have lived or journeyed throughout the Empire. For that I am very grateful.

I now quit altogether public affairs, and I lay down my burden. It may be sometime before I return to my native land, but I shall always follow the fortunes of the British race and Empire with profound interest, and if at any time in the future I can be found of service to His Majesty in a private station, I shall not fail.

And now we all have a new King. I wish him and you, his people, happiness and prosperity with all my heart. God Bless you all. God save the King.

Queen Mary was listening with her other sons at Royal Lodge when the historic speech came over the wireless. They were still together, late at night, when her eldest son, now no longer King, came back to say good-bye.

It was a personal message to the nation from her own hand that Queen Mary wrote of her distress at the thought that her son had "deemed it to be his duty to lay down his charge."

Always duty! Queen Mary was nearly 70 then. Now

she is 84. In the fifteen years that have passed since Mrs. Simpson stepped on the stage of history, Queen Mary, playing her own great, dignified role in the heart of the drama, has set eyes on her only once. That was at a party, early in the association, when Mrs. Simpson appeared as a casual acquaintance, a woman apparently of little importance.

Queen Mary has never received her, either as Mrs. Simpson, or as Duchess of Windsor. When the Duke of Windsor makes one of his brief visits to London he goes first, alone, to see his mother. Occasionally he has stayed overnight at Marlborough House. Usually, he goes then to stay with relatives and friends at their homes where his wife is received. Sometimes his visits take him near Fort Belvedere, the now empty and forlorn scene of his most poignant memories. But always he has gone first to Marlborough House to see his mother, Queen Mary.

```
┌─────────────────────────┐
│                         │
│   PART ELEVEN           │
│                         │
│                         │
└─────────────────────────┘
```

ON the evening of the Coronation of King George VI and Queen Elizabeth, Queen Mary, wearing her own crown as Queen Mother, stood between them on the balcony of Buckingham Palace and faced an ocean of happy, upturned faces that filled the Mall and every inch of space in front of the Palace. The little Princesses, wearing their Coronets, stood in front of the two Queens, and gaily waved their hands to the joyous throng.

Much of the cheering that came up from the crowds was for the Princesses. It came in great gusts, and, above all the tumult, names could be heard. Over and over again, the King and Queen acknowledged the acclamation of their people. Then a group would start up a call for the Princesses, who beamed their delight.

And then came a shout, "Queen Mary!" At once it spread through the crowd like a wind through a corn field, until all were hailing the woman who had been their Queen for more than twenty-five years, and now, invested in new dignity, seemed a nobler figure than ever.

Those standing near Queen Mary saw her eyes light up with that look of pleased surprise that they knew so well. It seemed to say, "But surely this is not for me?" And everyone then saw her stretch forth her hands towards her son and her daughter-in-law, as if to say: "These are your King and Queen. Love them as you have loved me."

For a long time they stood on the balcony, facing the throng. After their hurried dinner, they were called back to receive renewed acclaim.

By then the little Princesses had gone to bed. It had been a long and tiring day, in the processions, in the Abbey, and on the balcony for such young children. But the people in the streets were not tired. That was the night when Britain forgot to go to bed.

Many of them had been up all the night before, camping in the open on stools or cushions all along Whitehall and the Mall. The Coronation had brought the world to London. Visitors from overseas came in droves to witness the greatest spectacle of the age and to join in our celebrations.

Everyone old enough can remember the bonfires, the

flags, the streamers, the fireworks in every town and village, the Coronation rock, the Coronation hats and neckties and the "street parties" at which neighbors gathered to feast and dance and sing all night.

"You British people are nice, but so solemn," a foreign diplomat's wife once said to me. "You don't know how to make a *fiesta*." I suppose she meant that, unlike the people of Southern climes, we do not see in every event of the calendar an excuse for processions, noise and general letting off of steam.

She should have seen us at Coronation time. She would have realized that when we do find occasion to let ourselves go we make a *fiesta* so memorably colossal that it reverberates in history.

For Queen Mary, the Coronation was in many ways the culmination of the lifework of herself and her husband. Pageantry and crowds were nothing new to her. She had been one of the two principal figures in all the most spectacular Royal events of the century.

Her memory may have flashed back to the great Durbar at Delhi, which was really an extension, overseas, of the festivities of the Coronation of King George V and herself.

To Delhi they took their Coronation robes. In the procession entering the new Indian capital, King George V rode on his horse, but Queen Mary, "beautifully dressed in cream lace, a large hat with blue and cream feathers on fair hair, the Blue of the Garter slung across her shoulder and the great fan and umbrella over her head, sat, superbly erect as usual, alone in the carriage; her . . . gorgeousness excited the breathless admiration of the crowds."

The Imperial Camp, covering twenty-five square miles, held 300,000 people in 40,000 tents. The huge Amphitheater in which the Royal reception was held contained 12,000 people, with 18,000 troops facing the two silver thrones, and, on the Mound beyond, more than 50,000 spectators.

"May and I," wrote King George, "were photographed before we started, in our robes . . . with a new Crown made for India which cost £60,000, which the Indian Government is going to pay for."

Queen Mary wore her own Crown, with the Koh-in-Noor diamond and the famous emeralds flashing in the Indian sunshine. Her richly embroidered gown was gold and green, and a purple velvet mantle bordered with ermine hung from her shoulders. She and the King sat side by side on the thrones, while Princes paid homage, procession after procession passed, and guns roared.

From India Queen Mary brought back innumerable souvenirs of exquisite Indian workmanship. I have seen some of them in a large, glass-fronted cabinet in the picturesque Royal School in Windsor Great Park. Many others have been given by Queen Mary to school museums in all parts of the country, and thousands of children must have seen them and learned their history.

All the Oriental splendour of the Delhi Durbar must be a wonderful memory for Queen Mary. For her and her husband to be hailed almost as gods in a land so far away must have been deeply moving.

But how much more profoundly touching it was, on the evening of the Coronation of her son and his wife, to have them and their two lovely children with her on the balcony, and to realize that the hundreds of thousands of faces before her were those of her own people!

If she did think of the Durbar then, I am sure that some of the little details came to her mind. For example, on the voyage home from India, the ship's band played over and over again the King's favorite tune—Hermann Finck's "In the Shadows," which had become all the rage at home.

Queen Mary is fond of the popular music of those times, such as *The Arcadians* and *The Chocolate Soldier.*

Those must have been happy years, just before the Great War, when few people believed that there would ever be a war, much less have imagined what a world war would mean.

King George and Queen Mary (she in gold brocade) went to the Palace Theater to see Henry Tate and George Robey. They had often been to theaters, but this was Their Majesties first visit to a music hall, and it was a great event for Variety to receive a visit from Their Majesties.

And about that time, people were beginning to realize

that King George and Queen Mary were striking out on a line of their own. Queen Mary in particular had always liked to go among working people and see the conditions in which they lived and worked. Soon after the Coronation they made a series of industrial visits. Royalty had done that before of course, but differently.

When Queen Victoria visited a steel works in Yorkshire, the place was so transformed, with trees stuck in artificial banks, the steel covered in turf, and fairy lights everywhere, that the Queen, driving through the yard in a State landau for a few minutes, could have had no idea of what really went on in a steel mill.

But King George and Queen Mary, paying their frequent visits to factories, first insisted that the work should not be interrupted, and always had presented to them, not only the directors, but many of the workers in the various departments.

Soon the King and Queen were taking tea with a miner's wife in South Wales, visiting the industries of Yorkshire and Staffordshire.

Once, after a long day's tour of a mining district, they received the news of a disastrous explosion at Cadeby Colliery. Instead of merely sending a message of sympathy, they went by car to the spot, to see what help they could give.

When Queen Mary saw the weeping women at the pithead and heard the full story of the tragedy, tears streamed down her cheeks.

> *"Kind, kind and gentle is she;*
> *Kind is our Mary!"*

That is what the glass-blowers of Stairport sang when Queen Mary visited them at their work. And I heard it sung in the streets on that never-to-be-forgotten night of the Coronation of King George VI and Queen Elizabeth.

Not long after their own Coronation, King George V and Queen Mary went to Berlin for the wedding of the Duke of Cumberland and the Kaiser's only daughter.

There may have been a thought in the Queen's mind that such a marriage, and the festivities surrounding it, might help to drive away the tiny war cloud that even then was casting a shadow. At least, it was generally felt that it might keep the Kaiser, for a time, from his favorite sport of saber-rattling. And certainly he was affable enough at the wedding.

King George danced with the bride and Queen Mary with the groom, after which bride and groom danced with the whole company of Princes and Princesses, and, as a final gesture, pieces of the bride's garter, bearing the arms of the bridal pair, were distributed among the guests.

Possibly the piece of garter that Queen Mary received is not among the great collection of souvenirs that she has treasured: but we do know that she never throws anything of significance away.

For our King and Queen in Berlin, only an ordinary police escort was needed, but for the Czar of Russia the whole length of the railway line over which he traveled was guarded by troops, the railway stations were closed, and a large staff of Russian secret police surrounded their ruler.

Queen Mary had had another experience of the contrast between British freedom and Continental restraint. She must have remembered vividly the bomb explosion which marred the wedding day of her cousin, Princess Ena of Battenberg, and King Alfonso at Madrid.

King George and Queen Mary, as Prince and Princess of Wales, were in the procession returning to the Royal Palace after the ceremony; and this is what happened, in the Prince's own words.

"Our carriage was just in front of the one in which Queen Christina and Aunt Beatrice were driving and they were just ahead of Alfonso and Ena, who were at the end of the procession.

"Just before our carriage reached the Palace, we heard a loud report and thought it was the first gun of a salute. We soon learned, however, that when about 200 yards from the Palace, in a narrow street, the Calle Mayor, a bomb was thrown from an upper window at the carriage of the King and Queen.

"It fell between the wheel horses and the front of the carriage, killing about 20 people and wounding 50 or 60, mostly officers and soldiers.

"Thank God! Alfonso and Ena were not touched,

though covered with glass from the broken windows. The Marquesa Torlosa and her niece were killed. . . . Of course the bomb was thrown by an anarchist, supposed to be a Spaniard, and of course they let him escape. I believe the Spanish police and detectives are about the worst in the world."

Three days later the would-be assassin shot a policeman and then himself in a village near Madrid.

Queen Mary has always loved Paris, and the Parisians loved her. *"Qu'elle est belle!"* they cried on that Spring morning in 1914 when she drove through the Paris streets and out through the Bois de Boulogne on the State visit which could well have been a sign to the world that Britain would fight beside France if ever war came—and it was less than four months away.

President Poincaré of France presented to Queen Mary a beautiful silver mirror.

"I hope Your Majesty, that it will always reflect a happy face," he said.

"As long as I am in Paris, Monsieur le Président, the mirror will certainly reflect smiles and happiness," Queen Mary replied.

In a pale blue crêpe de soie dress, open sufficiently at the neck to show a superb rope of pearls, and a hat with a trimming of ostrich plumes, shading from the tone of the dress to a bluish white, our Queen Mary was hailed as *"Le printemps même"*—Springtime itself. And the general verdict of Paris was, *"Elle a son chic à elle"*— she has a chic of her own.

And yet, as we all know, she does not change her way of dress to suit the whims of fashion. In Windsor, there is a shop that proudly displays in a glass case a small, black, jet-covered bonnet that was made in the shop for Queen Victoria. Queen Mary also has hats made at this shop. Her exquisite flower-trimmed toques are known all over the world.

I myself am particularly fond of a hat which Queen Mary once admired. It was a toque (of course) and a very gay one, made of red currants with clusters of small red velvet roses, the whole creation having gossamer-red veiling. It drew a smile and a twinkle from Queen Mary when she saw me wearing it.

But a crown becomes her best of all. Three Coronations she has seen in Westminster Abbey—and one of them her own. At the Coronation of her son King George VI and Queen Elizabeth, Queen Mary saw her own life work crowned.

While the story of "The Little Princesses" was appearing in *Woman's Own,* an American magazine printed an article entitled, "Why does England have a King?" by a brilliant British writer.

He pointed out that "we set the ordinary man in the most exalted place of all, and require the extraordinary men to bow down and acknowledge themselves his servants." He wrote of "the ordinary man and the extraordinary charge." He went on to explain the duties and privileges that will be Princess Elizabeth's when, by God's grace, she becomes Queen of England.

It was all true enough, and perhaps it was the best explanation that could be given to citizens of a Republic, concerning an institution that must seem strange to them. How could they be brought to see that with us the Royal Family are more than an institution, but human, personal, intimate and very dear? And far from "ordinary?"

Fifty years ago, people in England were asking the same question, "Why do we have a Queen?" The great Joseph Chamberlain, father of Neville Chamberlain, began his political career as an avowed Republican, as many Radicals called themselves in those days.

Why is Republicanism, as a political aim, dead in Britain to-day? Not because Kings and Queens are less important than in the days when they ruled by force, or when they took sides in politics, but because they are now far more important.

Because they have made themselves loved.

The relations between the British people and their Royal Family have become a matter of real love and devotion. Early in this story, I told of Queen Mary's rapt expression at the Coronation of King Edward VII, and of her answer to a friend who asked her what she had been thinking about.

"What it all meant," she said, "—of the past."

How deep must have been her thoughts, how poignant her memories, when she stood on the balcony with King George VI and Queen Elizabeth and the Princesses, and felt the waves of affection flow upwards towards them?

Perhaps she thought of King Edward. In the twenty-six years since her own Coronation Queen Mary had seen thrones overturned, kingdoms swept away, countries invaded and frontiers obliterated. All that had changed, but the throne remained, established more firmly than ever in the people's hearts.

In the very years of her husband's coming to the throne, there was an attempt to blacken his character by scandal. A malicious report was circulated that the King, during his service in the Royal Navy, had contracted a marriage in Malta with the daughter of an Admiral. The King, with characteristic courage, went into a court of law and sued a man named Mylius for libel. At the trial it was proved that the Prince and the lady in question had never been in Malta at the same time. Mylius was sentenced to twelve months' imprisonment.

"The whole story is a damnable lie," wrote the King in his diary. "It has been in existence for over twenty years and I trust now that this will settle it once and for all."

It did. The domestic life of King George and Queen Mary already had set a pattern, and soon was to become a model to the world. Yet during her husband's reign, there was hardly a year without a crisis of some sort—political, economic or military.

Queen Mary was at her husband's side through the First World War, the depression that followed, the

General Strike, the financial collapse and slump, and the rise of Hitler. No King had had such an eventful reign.

Within a few months after the death of King George V, there came a crisis that involved the Throne itself. It was precisely then that the people realized, not for the first time but more clearly than ever before, what Queen Mary meant to them and what the Nation owed to her.

Although as Queen Mother she had not the smallest official part to play in the Government of the country, although she could not constitutionally utter one word that might influence the King and his Ministers, this lone widow was the one person to whom the people could look for a lead. Her calm example and her very presence had a steadying effect, and came from the confidence and trust that she and King George V had built up through the years.

They had brought the Throne close to the people, not by any sacrifice or surrender of their own dignity, but by maintaining it, and heightening it, and so setting an example. They brought something new and fine to Kingship—something more than the mere popularity that could be gained by winning horse-races or even wars.

That was what Queen Mary was handing on when, after the Coronation of King George VI and Queen Elizabeth, she stretched out her hands to them on the balcony. And the people knew exactly what she meant.

PART TWELVE

ON that night in 1940 when Princess Elizabeth broadcast to the boys and girls of the Empire and then called her little sister, Princess Margaret, to the microphone to say, "Goodnight, children," their grandmother, Queen Mary, sat and listened in her sitting room at Badminton, the Gloucestershire home of the Duke and Duchess of Beaufort.

"I was moved to tears," Queen Mary said to me afterwards. "It was so natural and unaffected."

And more than once she has told me how, during her enforced stay at Badminton, she pined for the company of her family, and especially her little granddaughters, knowing, as she said, "that I should find a great difference in them, in all kinds of ways."

Only twice during those war years was she able to go to Windsor, where the children were. In 1941, for the confirmation of Princess Elizabeth, and again on

August 29th, 1942, the night before the funeral of her son, the Duke of Kent.

Queen Mary did not want to go to Badminton. It was only because the King and Queen persuaded her that she would cause anxiety to them and everyone else if she stayed in London that she consented to go. Then it became a duty.

I know from what she has told me that she herself suffered great anxiety for the King and Queen in London and the children at Windsor, especially at times when bombs were falling.

Queen Mary was at the morning service in Sandringham village church when she heard over the loud speakers Mr. Neville Chamberlain's announcement that we were at war with Germany. Next morning, after a night of alarms, she, with her lady-in-waiting, Lady Cynthia Colville, and her equerry, the Hon. John Coke, set out on the cross-country journey that had been planned months before.

It must have been a sad ride for Queen Mary, remembering how, in the First World War, when she was twenty-five years younger and Queen of England, she had been able to plunge at once into the thick of the work.

On that fateful August Monday of 1914, she stood with the King and the young Prince of Wales on the balcony of Buckingham Palace and witnessed a great demonstration of the people's loyalty and affection.

Four days later she was at Tidworth, bidding farewell to her own regiment, the 18th Hussars, on the eve of its sailing for France with the first British Expeditionary Force. But already she had begun to put in motion her plan, conceived long before, to bring the women of Britain together in an organized war effort.

The present generation may not realize what a great part Queen Mary played in making the nation aware of the importance of women's work in wartime. It was something new in history.

It laid the foundation on which much of the home-front organization of the Second World War was built.

Queen Mary has never been a feminist, in the ordinary, political sense of the word. She showed no approval when the Suffragettes chained themselves to railings, went on hunger-strikes in prison and made heroic figures of themselves in a cause that everyone knows to have been just.

King George V simply did not understand them. "I don't know what we are coming to," he said when a debutante at Court went down on her knees before him and shouted, "For God's sake, Your Majesty." What Queen Mary thought of it all is not recorded; but we do know that from the very beginning of the First World War she saw how important women's work in wartime would be.

She threw all her energy into the task of enlisting a voluntary and enthusiastic army of women workers in national service. For that purpose she gathered round her women leaders of all parties, including Socialists and others who had fought in the Suffragette cause.

"All that we women can do for them, our soldiers will need," said Queen Mary to Lady Bertha Dawkins, her lady-in-waiting, on the first day of the war. "We must have everything ready.

"I do not want to have that state of things which prevailed during the Boer War, with people sending just what they liked, without relation to the real needs of our soldiers, without organization. It entails too much waste and loss of time. "Let us strive for central organizations from which to control and direct. Soon there will be thousands of women wanting to do something to help and not knowing what to do. Let us be ready for them."

So Queen Mary became the leader of women on the Home Front. Her Needlework Guild, of which her mother, the Duchess of Teck, had been President, had been founded in Victorian times, "to distribute clothing, household linen and other articles suitable for the sick and the poor among the hospitals, charitable societies and parishes in London." At the outbreak of war it became a vast production plant and clearing house for wartime needs. An army of women, all volunteers, were set to work.

Immediately after the retreat from Mons, early in the war, the Secretary of State for War begged Queen Mary to let him have 200,000 sweaters and 200,000 pairs of socks for the troops. She saw that they were delivered in time.

Friary Court, St. James's Palace, where formerly Royal levees were held, was lent to the Guild by the King, and soon the magnificent rooms, including that in which King Charles I spent the night before his beheading, looked like a department store.

The Tapestry room, the Armoury, Queen Anne's Drawing-rooms, and the Henry VIII Color Court—indeed every part of the Palace except the Throne Room —all were filled with clothing and comforts, not only for the troops but also for Belgian refugees and British people who had been impoverished by war.

Gifts poured in from America and the Dominions, where many branches of the Guild were formed to augment the work of the 630 branches at home. In the first two years of the war, nearly 4,000,000 garments passed through Friary Court.

But at the very outset of the work a serious problem arose. What of the seamstresses and other women workers who might be thrown out of employment by this army of volunteers?

Why should they suffer because of the efforts of those whom a woman leader called "the well-meaning and well-to-do, who were seized with a perfect epidemic of needlework and so competed feverishly with unemployed women by the socks, shirts and other garments that they turned out for the soldiers?"

Queen Mary, having been all her life a student of

industrial problems, was one of the first to see the threat. While a deputation of women workers was preparing to appeal to her, she made the first move. Politicians had refused to listen to others; they had to listen to Queen Mary.

How she solved the problem has been told fully in a book written by Kathleen Woodward twenty-seven years ago; the most illuminating part of the story concerns Queen Mary's relation with women Labor leaders, such as Mary Macarthur and Margaret Bondfield, who until then had, to say the least, little sympathy with the institution of royalty. Until they met Queen Mary!

After her first meeting with the Queen, Mary Macarthur went back to her Socialist colleagues with a shout of delight.

"Here," she cried, "is someone who can and who means to help!" The two Marys met often after that, and Mary Macarthur often told her friends: "The point is that the Queen simply does understand and grasp the whole situation from the Trade Union point of view. She does understand."

Margaret Bondfield found the same thing. "Queen Mary's competent understanding," she said, "her entire sincerity, her utter simplicity, are absolutely unlike the 'sympathetic interest' of so many ladies. With her you know precisely where you are."

Mrs. J. R. Clynes, wife of the Food Controller, a Socialist, told Miss Woodward how she found Queen

Mary one day at Windsor sitting on a couch, "knitting, knitting, knitting; and never once did she stop the working of those fingers; while she told me how she could not take her mind from the memory of some men she had been visiting who had been gassed."

Mrs. Clynes asked her about the socks the Queen was knitting. "Are they for your boys, Ma'am?" she asked.

No; they were for the Needlework Guild; for any soldiers. But even then they could have reached one or other of Queen Mary's sons—Edward, in the Grenadier Guards, soon to fight at Passchaendale, or Albert, in H.M.S. *Collingwood,* to fight at Jutland.

For months on end during the first war hardly a day passed without Queen Mary's visiting hospitals and talking with the wounded. When she went to France with the King in 1917 she had heard of the "joy rides" of some privileged visitors, and she wanted none of that. Instead, she insisted on visiting men who had suffered ghastly wounds. She saw war at its ugliest.

The Dowager Countess of Airlie, Lady of the Bedchamber to Queen Mary, has testified: "However many hospitals Her Majesty visited a day, she spoke to every single patient in them. Not a solitary one did she miss." And everyone wondered "how on earth it was humanly possible for a woman to sustain from day to day what Her Majesty was called on to sustain, to go through what she did go through."

Not everyone will remember now the slanders that

were set afoot about the Women's Army Auxiliary Corps in the first war. Queen Mary effectively scotched them by becoming the Commander-in-Chief of the WAACs on the very day of the official citation telling of their bravery during the great drive of April, 1918.

"I am afraid," said the Queen, "that I cannot do much actual work, but I will do everything in my power." What she did was to put a new spirit of pride into the Corps. An American headquarters commander paid the Corps this tribute:

"The conduct of these young women under surroundings absolutely new to them, working in daily association with men from another army, and whom they had never seen before, has been such as to gain for them the admiration and commendation of all persons, both civil and military, in this community. . . .

"They have proved themselves a credit to their officers, to their chief who organized and commands their corps, and to their country."

Whatever the task, Queen Mary was ready for it. Lord Devonport, the first wartime Food Controller said: "Of all the practical women in this world—including my own wife—there is not a more practical, a more understanding, a more helpful woman than Queen Mary."

She foresaw the need of food rationing, and she and King George V introduced austerity for their own family (but not the servants) long before rationing became compulsory. During King George's wartime absences from the country, Queen Mary shouldered extra duties.

Hearing that General Joffre, the French Commander-in-Chief, had come to London and was being allowed to leave without an invitation to Buckingham Palace, she insisted on having a talk with him and sending a message to the French army and nation.

At that time King George was on a bed of pain in France. His horse had reared and fallen on him, and his pelvis was fractured. For several days he could not sleep without drugs. Many people believe that, after the accident, he was never as strong as before.

At the beginning of the war, when Queen Mary was forty-seven, her hair was still golden. At the end it was grey.

With such memories of the war of 1914–1918 vividly revived by the sirens of September 3rd, 1939, Queen Mary must have gone to Badminton with a heavy heart. But she did have the satisfaction of knowing that the spadework she had done in the first war would not have to be done again. There would be no need, this time, to rouse the country to the need for women's hands and brains. Women were important in wartime, and everyone knew it, thanks most of all to Queen Mary. The machinery that she had brought into being was ready for use again.

And now, at seventy-two, she was an evacuee in a

country village, far from the London she loved, with its hospitals, picture galleries, antique shops and theaters. Far from her own family.

As the young Duchess of York, mistress of York Cottage, Sandringham, she had known country life, but never as intimately as she would come to know it at Badminton. It is a fine old house, set in the midst of lovely countryside.

Queen Mary had stayed there before as the guest of the Duke and Duchess of Beaufort, but she had not explored it, as she set out to do as soon as she arrived.

As she walked round the house and through the park she was amused and charmed to see that a personal bodyguard, composed of one company of troops from the Gloucestershire Regiment, the Rifle Brigade and the Royal Berkshire Regiment, was quartered there. She soon came to know these men well, and also the four dispatch riders from the Royal Corps of Signals who were attached to her service.

If the Germans had landed, whether as an army or as raiders, they might have tried to capture Queen Mary and carry her off as a hostage—possibly by air. The bodyguard was there to prevent such an attempt. The task of the dispatch riders would have been to guide her through the countryside to one of several safer places that had been chosen beforehand.

For six years the little village of Badminton was Queen Mary's "home town." She knew its little shops, and the people behind the counters. She stopped at cottage gates to admire the gardens and chat with her neighbors, the villagers; and sometimes she dropped in at a cottage for a cup of tea.

She came to know about crops, and to discuss with farmers the problems of soil and weather. As a member of the local pig club, she raised her own pig, and dutifully surrendered her bacon coupons.

"Rations only" was the rule at Badminton. When sugar ran out everyone in the household had to use saccharine. The house was cold and damp, because there was not enough fuel to keep the central heating plant going, but Queen Mary refused to accept more than her share of the counted-out lumps of coal.

It may have been the search for fuel that put in her mind the idea of clearing up parts of the estate that had become overgrown with trees and bushes. Or it may have been her instinct for tidiness. At any rate, as she walked in the grounds early one morning she came upon a clump of tangled woods, matted with undergrowth, and there and then the idea was born.

In the village were a number of evacuee children, mostly from Birmingham, who were finding country life dull. Queen Mary asked them how they would like to come and help her.

In old clothes and thick gloves, she led the way, and soon she and the children were tearing down ivy and clearing undergrowth. The children's enthusiasm did not last long. As the work grew harder most of them dropped out.

But by then Queen Mary had enlisted quite an army of workers, including the soldiers of her own Guard, members of her household, villagers, and every visitor who came to Badminton—including the King, the Duke and Duchess of Gloucester, and the late Duke of Kent.

"Wouldn't you like something to do?" she would ask a visitor who seemed to be idle after breakfast; and that afternoon at two o'clock he would find himself wielding a billhook, a saw or an axe in one of the "wooding parties." By the end of the war, 120 acres of scrubland had been cleared and made useful in this way.

That was only one of Queen Mary's many wartime activities.

She knitted pullovers, mufflers and socks for the troops. She dealt personally with a daily heap of correspondence. She organized weekly movies for villagers and troops at the great house, and often sat with her neighbors at plays and films in the village hall.

Just as it always had been with her, she made good use of every minute. More than once, in visiting one or other of the canteens in the neighborhood, she went behind the counter, rolled up her sleeves and served tea to soldiers.

Immediately after the evacuation of Dunkirk she motored to the village of Dursley to meet and talk with men who had been brought home from the beaches.

Stained and dirty, in ragged battledress, they cheered Queen Mary. To each of the 135 men she gave a shirt and a pair of socks that she had bought at Bath and brought with her.

In many ways she was quite as busy as she had been in the first war. She made scores of unofficial visits to nearby factories and talked with the workers.

Few bombs came near Badminton, but Bristol was only seventeen miles away, and night after night, during the assaults on that city, explosions shook the earth and the sky was lit by bomb flashes and the glow of fires.

On the morning after one raid on Bristol, Queen Mary drove there with her daughter, the Princess Royal, and the Duke of Beaufort to see the damage and talk with the Civil Defence workers.

In her many inspections of troops, she did not forget the A.T.S. at Salisbury, the W.R.N.S. at Bristol and the W.A.A.F. at airfields in the Badminton area. There she saw what her own Women's Auxiliary Army Corps of the first war had grown to be.

Her contacts with the forces were by no means restricted to parades and inspections. When she motored in the country, it was a regular thing for her to give lifts to men and women in Service uniform. Some of them at first refused to believe their eyes when they saw who had picked them up. When they assured themselves that they were not dreaming, but were actually sitting beside Queen Mary in the royal car, they still felt that they would never be able to persuade anyone else that it was true. Who would believe a soldier who said that he had "thumbed a lift" from Queen Mary?

So Queen Mary had hundreds of little metal medallions made, bearing her Royal Cipher and Crown, as souvenirs by which her wartime passengers could prove that they had ridden with her.

By that time the United States was in the war, and many of the airfields near Badminton were filled with American airmen. Mr. Louis Wulff, M.V.O., has told how one twenty-two year old American soldier, Private Ora A. Foster, from Michigan, thumbing a lift back to camp, found himself sitting beside a very charming grey-haired lady and telling her all about his home town, his family and his views on the war, life in Britain, and things in general.

"Near the end of the journey, his hostess in the car asked for a package to be passed to her. 'Yes, Your Majesty,' came the reply, and young Ora began to wonder who she was.

" 'You don't know who I am, do you?' the lady asked.

" 'There you have me beat,' Ora replied.

"Then Queen Mary smilingly revealed her identity and gave him one of her medallions."

Queen Mary saw much of the Americans after that, and learned from them of the differences and similarities between their way of life and ours. She visited their wounded in hospitals at Bath and elsewhere, and she saw her first baseball match when two U.S. army teams met at Clifton.

It is quite a mistake to think of Queen Mary's war years at Badminton as a quiet exile, away from the world of strife. They were very busy years, and she was very much in the world, meeting people, finding work to do every day, keeping in touch with everything that was going on.

At Windsor Castle I had many messages from her, mostly about the Princesses, and the only complaint she ever made was about her absence from them and her family.

How she must have missed them on her six wartime birthdays! Instead of the Princesses bringing posies, there were telegrams from them on her breakfast table, and from her neighbors, the village boys and girls, a bunch of simple flowers picked in their cottage gardens.

I wish I could have been there to see Queen Mary's delight when Queen Elizabeth took the Princesses to Badminton in May, 1944. In the evening, the two Queens and the two Princesses attended the service in the village church, and then joined in the Rogationtide procession round the village, singing hymns while the vicar prayed for a blessing on the crops.

The worst of the war was over then. Within a year Queen Mary would be getting ready to say farewell to her many friends in Badminton and the countryside around. I think she was as sorry to leave as she had been to go.

But she was coming back to London, to her own Marlborough House, where she and King George had first met and played as children, where she could gather about her again all the personal belongings that she treasured, where she would spend many happy years, serene, tranquil, yet never idle, living according to the standard that she had set in a message from Buckingham Palace on March 23rd, 1923:

"Remember that life is made up of loyalty; loyalty to your friends; loyalty to things beautiful and good; loyalty to the country in which you live; loyalty to your King; and, above all, for this holds all other loyalties together, loyalty to God."

On May 26, 1951, Queen Mary entered her eighty-fifth year, with that undiminished responsiveness to life which has marked all her years and the vitality with which to enjoy them amazingly sustained. Not since the Norman Conquest in 1066 has any British King or Queen—regnant, consort or dowager—reached so many birthdays.

Seeing her today, it is hard to appreciate that she was born as long ago as 1867, when the most terrible civil war in written history had just ended and the thirty-seven States of the American Union were starting the slow reconstruction of their ravaged land.

That was the year—symbolic to my mind—when the

Atlantic cable went into operation, spanning 3,000 miles of ocean and drawing closer together the English-speaking nations. I like to think that, in her own special way, Queen Mary has also linked these countries, and the wonderful *gros point* carpet which became known to us all as Queen Mary's Carpet is a symbol of that achievement.

Her interest in needlework goes back to the early thirties, when she took instruction in the ancient art of embroidery, which has been practiced in Britain for nearly 1,000 years, at the Royal School of Needlework in London.

The school was founded by a daughter of Queen Victoria, Princess Christian, when little Princess May was only five years old. As Queen Mary, she had seen the school's work in some of the most beautiful embroidery on the Coronation canopies and robes when she and her husband were crowned in Westminster Abbey in 1911.

When she began plying her needles on Queen Mary's Carpet, she had already made a smaller one for her own use; it is in the Marlborough House drawing room now. The school submitted the designs, based on eighteenth century English tapestries, for the larger carpet.

She originally intended it as a gift for another member of the royal family. But when, after the war, Britain's economic plight became desperate, she made up her mind to present the carpet to the nation for sale as a royal "dollar export." The money would help to buy new machines for Britain's factories from North America, and she hoped to set an example for her people by stressing the sacrifices we all must make to ensure the success of the drive for dollars.

In 1948, six exquisite chair seat covers which she had made and given to a nursing organisation were sold in the United States for $10,000; they are kept now among the art treasures of the Metropolitan Museum in New York City.

Queen Mary started work on the carpet in the early days of the war when the German bombers were droning over her country. She chose the hundred pastel colours with special care—the soft beiges, the delicate grays, the blues, turquoises, mauves and ambers for every individual flower and leaf, bird and blossom in the design.

In my memory I can see her sitting by the tall windows of Marlborough House, sewing bag at hand, pursuing the intricate tracery of patterns, as soon as breakfast, letter writing and Palace business was completed. She was following a long tradition where British Queens are concerned, starting with Margaret, Anglo-Saxon Queen of Scotland in the tenth century, down through the centuries to Queen Victoria. In some ancient English palaces and manorhouses, one can still inspect the work of Catherine of Aragon and her daughter, Mary I ("Bloody Mary").

Our Queen Mary worked as they must have done. The rows of wools, four hundred and eighty different kinds by the time the carpet was finished, were ranged in parade-ground order beside her chair. Seated straight-backed and serene, she would choose the color she wanted, snip off a length of it with her silver-gilt scissors kept in a worn leather case, swiftly thread a needle without the aid of spectacles, and make another stitch while I watched and listened and talked with her.

She worked regularly until lunch and then again in the late evening, six to seven hours a day. Slowly but surely the tapestry grew, four stitches a minute in her ceaseless skill. The first of the twelve panels was completed in May, 1941, and she added the finishing touch of a true artist—her signature "Mary R." and the date. Eight years and one million stitches after she commenced her womanly, queenly task, Queen Mary's Carpet was ready to be shipped across the 3,000 miles of ocean which it spanned in spirit, aboard the Cunard liner which proudly bears her name.

Except for the work of joining together the twelve panels, which she entrusted to the Royal School of Needlework, every stitch in the carpet was hers. After its first display in New York's Metropolitan Museum, and on television programs, newsreels and in hundreds of newspapers and magazines, it was taken on an exhibition tour of North America, protected in its special chest of solid English oak lined with stainless steel and equipped with handmade locks, produced by the King's own safe manufacturers.

Great crowds stood in line, often for hours, to win a glimpse of the carpet until, finally, Queen Mary's personal contribution to Britain's recovery campaign was sold for $100,000 over and above the proceeds of subsequent showings and collections, to the Canadian members of the Imperial Order of the Daughters of the Empire.

Characteristically, the Queen who had turned even her hobby into a means of aiding her country and her people, had meantime begun working on another carpet, stoically ignoring the sciatica which causes her increasing pain these days. "I never knew if I would live to finish the first," she said, "so there is no reason why I should not start a second."

As her years lengthen, her tranquillity seems to increase. Among the thousands of telegrams, bouquets of flowers and other gifts of heart-felt affection which greet her every birthday, she particularly looks for the message from the Lord Mayor on behalf of the people of London, the city close to her love. Last year her reply brought tears to my eyes as I read it; I have spoken to many people about it, and they all felt the same wave of emotion. Of the citizens of London, she said, "It is always a joy to me to receive an assurance that I still hold a place in their affection and to know that they remember me on my birthday."

Today, Queen Mary has sometimes to use a wheel chair or, in the damp London winter, is confined to the home she loves. On November 11, 1950, she missed the Cenotaph Service, commemorating Armistice Day, for the first time. But the previous summer she spent five and a half hours at Wimbledon watching the tennis.

She still takes on a volume of work which would tire anyone half her age. She attended, with keen customary interest, the Festival of Britain ceremonies, although she sat in her wheel chair part of the time.

Her memory remains uncannily keen. At Buckingham Palace Garden Parties she will recognize someone she has not seen for a quarter of a century. Those of us who see her have sought in vain for adequate words to express and sum up what she means to us. A Cockney woman, during a recent visit to Queen Mary to a working men's club in the East End of London, came as close as any of us to success when she said, "She is every inch a Queen."

But here, as I close my notebook at the end of this story of love, my eye catches a phrase I jotted down years ago, a tribute paid to the Queen Mother.

"Hers is the perfect simplicity and serenity outside of time."